JOURNEYS
IN DARKNESS AND LIGHT

REBECCA WEISS

www.globalbookpublisher.com
2004

CONTENTS

Comments on *Journeys in darkness and light*

"A moving and powerful story, told in a straight and unsentimental way."
Berit Skogsberg, publisher, Sweden

"Well written and interesting—I was especially shaken by the chapter on Skå, the children's village, which is described as a trip to hell."
Arbetarbladet Newspaper, Finland, Aug. 2004

"This book is unique, fascinating, brave, passionate, incredibly honest, and truly universal. It is a very real presentation of a relevant spiritual life that can speak to a lot of people. I am very excited about the book."
Maggy Graham, editor, Florida

"It is written in a restrained style that has a strong effect on the reader. Above all it is a piece of Swedish cultural history."
Broderskap Newspaper, Sweden, March 2004

"I couldn't put it down. It is exciting and humorous and sparkles with life. I appreciate the simple and candid style of writing."
Molly Johnson, award-winning author, Sweden

"A truthful, honest and important book."
David Gaiman, business executive, England

"It gives hope and future to spirituality."
Noelle Saugout, documentary filmmaker, France

"Rebecca Weiss writes with courage and honesty about difficult subjects, and yet with respect for all involved. What a journey she has made in life. I am full of admiration."
Ingrid Sjöstrand, award-winning author, Sweden

"I was absolutely fascinated. There is so much love and insight in this book."
Peggy Oppenheim, artist, California

"The author shows a greatness and humbleness that few people have. Understanding and love shine through the pages."
Thomas Pettersson, director of a drug rehabilitation facility, Sweden

"I was so moved by this book. It feels like a sincere letter to friends, and an important message to everyone else."
Lenke Rothman, artist and author, Sweden

"The best book I ever read. It was so interesting and easy to read."
Sara Rizzardini, age 20, student, California

"I love *Journeys in darkness and light*! I felt a sense of peace when I finished it. It is real and human and I will treasure it forever."
Anita Welch, writer, Florida

"I couldn't put it down, and didn't want it to end. It is magnificent, and so close to my heart. I wish it was translated to Hebrew!"
Gali Halamish, artist, Israel

For Helga

INTRODUCTION

This is a book about journeys. It is not a consecutive autobiography, and long periods of my life have been left out. Journeys are the most exciting things in life—the inner ones as well as the outer in the physical world.

I am an artist, born and raised in Sweden, but now a U.S. resident. I have lived in many countries, traveled to many places, and have met some unique and outstanding people. I think my special combination of journeys, schools, friends and encounters, and my spiritual quest, might be of interest to others.

My mother was also an artist, well known in Scandinavia. My father was a painter, author and playwright and is internationally known in the world of theatre and literature. They were both extraordinary individuals who have deeply influenced my life. I want to show some aspects of them and of myself that others may not be aware of.

The chapters from my youth are written from the viewpoint I had at that time. I write what I remember. While I have tried to verify as many facts as I could, it was not always possible. If there are errors, I apologize.

Some names, places and details have been deliberately changed. Some sequences have been slightly simplified, to make them easier for readers to follow.

I have mainly written about friends from childhood and youth, or who are connected with certain journeys or important events in my life. Therefore some of my best friends have not been mentioned, but I treasure each one of them.

Above all I am grateful to my husband Stu, who gives me so much love and support, and to my mother Helga, who was an inspiration for all.

CORSICA

When I was four years old my mother Helga picked me up and took me to Corsica, an island in the Mediterranean Sea between France and Italy. Up to this point, she had left me with my grandparents or other people, because she was a free-spirited young artist who usually could not be bothered with children. She had recently divorced my father, Peter, who was an equally irresponsible young artist.

But now Helga and I were going away together. She was going to paint and write a book. Helga did speak French and Italian, as well as her native Swedish, but had no friends in Corsica and no idea where we would stay.

We arrived by ship in Bastia, a coastal town surrounded by high mountains. The houses were white with red tile roofs, and there were palm trees and eucalyptus along the boulevards. In this town Helga by chance encountered a middle-aged man who must have been a member of the Mafia. His eyes were green and he was dark and muscular. He always carried a gun and we were told he was a criminal, but he had a soft spot for women and children.

Helga called him the Robber, and I knew him by no other name. He owned a tiny, rundown hotel up in the mountains, above the beach. Since it was off-season the hotel was empty, and he invited us to stay there for free.

When we were settled in, the Robber gave Helga a loaded gun and left us to our own devices. He was often gone for several days in a row, and we never knew when he would return or what he did on his trips. "Business" he said when we asked. Helga slept with the gun under her pillow.

Weeks passed, while Helga painted, and I played in the bar of the hotel which was dark and smelled of wine and coffee. Sometimes I played in the garden, picking wildflowers or watching tadpoles in the pond. I also fell in love with the Robber's son, Nicola, who was in his late teens. Unlike his father, he was tall, blond and had blue eyes. He lived somewhere else, but frequently came to visit. It is remarkable how one can fall in love at the age of four, and experience much the same emotions that one feels later in life. Every time Nicola visited I would blush and giggle and my heart would pound.

We had hardly any money. A farmer who lived nearby gave us goat cheese and olives, and we picked cherries and mulberries from the trees. Sometimes the Robber cooked for us, spicy soups that he made from muraena-fish. He also fed me quinine, a medicine to prevent malaria. It was a nasty tasting powder and hard to swallow even when mixed with preserves. I still can recall the bitter taste of strawberry jam with quinine.

The Robber had no wife, but I don't think he had an affair with Helga. I think he just genuinely liked us and enjoyed our company.

One day the Robber decided to have a party. He invited everyone in the neighborhood and spent a whole day cooking. A stew of fish, clams, wine, olive oil, tomatoes, green peppers, garlic and herbs was made in a huge iron pot. I didn't like the stew at all, but the Robber seemed satisfied. He also produced his own wine with his bare hands and Helga said it was divine.

At sundown the guests arrived—whole families with children, grandparents, dogs and donkeys. I befriended Marie Josée, a five-year-old girl with red ribbons in her hair. Some people came on horseback, some in rowboats from down the coast. Soon the place was crowded and the guests ate and drank with great gusto. Nicola played the violin and a bearded man played the accordion and sang loudly in Italian.

The Robber ran around with his shirt open and a gun in his hand, shooting in the air. People danced wildly, mostly barefoot, and some collapsed on the floor. Helga, a blonde 5'10" woman, wore flowers in her hair and danced with men who were half a head shorter. I danced with Marie Josée.

When the summer season started the Robber needed all the hotel rooms for his guests. He then took Helga and me down to the beach and helped us build a hut out of branches from a eucalyptus tree. He gave us a blanket that was pierced by gunshots, and a clay pitcher we could use to fetch water from the well. We put a layer of fern on the ground to make it soft to sleep on. Helga could barely stretch out in the hut and it had no door. The scent of eucalyptus was intoxicating. Ever since then I have loved that scent.

A stray white dog joined us, and became our friend and protector. We named her Blanche. In the daytime I played with her on the beach, and at night she slept by my feet in the hut. Animals are truly wonderful. They have a goodness and innocence that you seldom find in humans.

It was a very peaceful time—one of the few happy periods of my childhood. We were completely alone on a deserted beach, but it never occurred to me to be afraid. Helga apparently was not afraid either or at least she didn't show it.

Later, when it was time to return to Sweden, we had to leave Blanche behind. We drove in an open car, and Blanche ran after the car for miles. It was a heartbreaking incident and I was inconsolable for a long time. I still don't understand how we could have been so cruel to Blanche.

Several decades later, I met another stray dog that was *not* being abandoned. This was Carmelito, whom friends of mine had found in the Texas desert. He became a permanent, beloved member of their family, and went with them wherever they traveled. In some roundabout way, that made me feel better about Blanche.

THE FIRST TRIP TO HELL

In Sweden in the 1950s there was a famous child psychologist named Gustav Jonsson. He ran a radio program giving advice to parents, and he founded a village for children called Skå. Children who were considered difficult, maladjusted or criminal were sent to Skå.

In the winter of 1951 when Helga was again abroad, my father Peter was supposed to take care of me. But he was preoccupied with his current mistress, and did not have time for me. Since he knew and admired Gustav Jonsson, he sent me to Skå.

There were only boys in the village, about fifty of them, aged eight to fifteen. I was six years old when I arrived, I was the only girl in the village, and among the few children there who were not criminal.

I was placed in a grey two-storey house where I shared a room with two boys, eight and ten years old. In the evenings they used to sit naked on their beds and openly masturbate. I had never seen anything like that, and it had an unpleasant, upsetting effect on me.

Since I was the youngest and weakest child, I was often bullied by the boys. This was the first time I had experienced physical violence and it petrified me. One day I decided to run away, and walked by myself on the road. A couple of boys found me, threw me to the ground and left me there freezing and crying.

I tried to seek refuge with the housemother who lived in my building. She was a tense and nervous young woman, and I noticed that she didn't want me around. No adults spoke to me and I had nowhere to go. The despair I felt at Skå is hard to describe. It was like sliding down a bottomless black hole. I remember clearly that I wanted to die.

Once I was awakened in the middle of the night. A group of older boys were standing around my bed. They started to touch me between my legs and said they were going to rape me. I don't fully remember what happened after that—the terror made me sort of black out. One would think that a child my age who hadn't had much sex education wouldn't know what was happening, but in some inexplicable way I knew *exactly* what it was about. The strange atmosphere in the room, the hoarse laughter and threatening voices of the boys, the odd expression in their eyes—it all created a deep horror inside me. I knew I should scream, try to wake up the housemother, try to get out of bed and run away, but I was paralyzed and unable to make a sound.

Eventually they walked away. They did not actually rape me, but from that time onward I was fearful of boys and men.

One day a boy slammed a door on my hand. A finger on my left hand got crushed, and I fainted with pain. This was the only time the housemother showed some interest in me— she quickly called an ambulance. I was rushed to a hospital, anesthetized and operated on. They managed to save the finger, but to this day it is scarred and malformed.

During the months at Skå I phoned Peter several times.

I begged him, weeping, to take me home. But he didn't, not even after I was hospitalized.

In 2001 I got an email from Staffan Lamm, Gustav Jonsson's son, who has published a book about his own troubled childhood. In the 1960s Staffan was a close friend of Peter and his wife Gunilla, and I often saw him in their home. Staffan told me in his email that he had seen a note I had sent to Peter while I was at Skå. I had made a drawing of a crying girl, with tears running down the whole page. In shaky, childlike letters I had written that Skå was horrible and that Peter must please come and get me.

How Peter could have left me there I have never understood. When Helga eventually returned to Sweden and found out what had happened, she was devastated. She immediately went out to Skå to pick me up. For decades she could not hear the word Skå without crying.

What I find the most serious is not that Peter left me at Skå, but that he never tried to make amends for it. Later in my life there were times when Peter had a chance to help me by showing tolerance and understanding. But he did not—on the contrary, he made my life a living hell during some of my adult years. *That* was the hardest thing to forgive.

JOURNEY OUT OF LIFE

Peter and Helga had left me with Peter's parents in 1944 when I was only three months old, and I stayed there for two years. My grandparents Franziska and Eugen Weiss were immigrants from Central Europe and were called Mutti and Daddy by both their children and grandchildren. They lived in Alingsås, a small town in western Sweden.

I don't remember much from these first years of my life. But in the old photos I look quite content holding Mutti's hand, and in Daddy's arms I look almost ecstatic. There was a special affinity between Daddy and me—I still feel it when I think of him.

In 1946 Peter and Helga took me back for a while. I have been told that I then refused to eat, refused to speak to them, and didn't even want them to look at me. In the mixture of German and Swedish I had heard from my grandparents I said: "nein titta" (no look) and turned my head away when Peter or Helga approached me.

After Alingsås I lived with Helga's mother Signe whom I did not feel close to at all. She was probably fond of me, but she had so many other grandchildren, and other interests. I had lost Helga and Peter, then Mutti and Daddy as well.

Perhaps these losses were the source of the sadness and insecurity I felt in my youth. I was frequently moved between different people and there was no stable adult I could trust. The experiences at Skå caused by far the worst damage. From that point on, I "moved out of life" and was no longer really present. But sometimes I think I was born unhappy.

I lived in a different world and saw people who did not exist. When I was in first grade a cousin asked me what my teacher looked like. I described my teacher in detail—she had long black curly hair and brown eyes. My cousin was very surprised and said there was no teacher in the school who looked anything like that. The next day when I looked closer at the teacher, I saw she had short blond hair and blue eyes. This was very confusing—I had been certain she was dark and brown-eyed.

There was also an imaginary friend whom I called Aling. He was my age and had curly black hair just like I thought my teacher had. He used to sit on a chair next to me and I got upset if someone tried to sit on that chair. "Can't you see that Aling is sitting there!" I shouted. Aling was more real to me than the actual people around me, and I had long conversations with him. Sometimes he would sing, monotone, haunting tunes. He was a great comfort, always caring and understanding, always there for me.

ALINGSÅS

After Skå I stayed with Helga for a few months. But she soon wanted to travel again, and I was sent back to my grandparents Mutti and Daddy. At this time they were in their late sixties. They had been thirteen years in Sweden but still spoke poor Swedish. Together they spoke German, and I learned this language by listening to them.

Mutti and Daddy used to live in Berlin, but because Daddy was Jewish, they and their children (Peter, Irene and Alexander) had to leave Germany. In 1938, after a couple of years in London and Prague, they came to Alingsås where Daddy had business connections. There Daddy became the president of a textile factory called Silfa.

Daddy was slim and of medium height. His eyes were blue and I thought his face was beautiful, even when he was an old man. He was always immaculately dressed in three-piece suits and ties. His thin grey hair was carefully combed, and his nails perfectly polished. Mutti was heavy, had a large bosom, and small feet. She called her feet "Autofüsschen," meaning they were too small to walk on, so she always had to travel by car. In her youth she had been an actress at the Max Reinhardt Theatre in Berlin, and even now she wore a fair amount of make-up, as though she were about to go on stage.

Her hair was still black with only a few strands of white, and her eyes were dark and glowing. She usually wore red nail-varnish, and smelled of powder and perfume.

They lived in a large, brown villa in the outskirts of Alingsås. In spite of its size it was called "Lillgården" which loosely translated means "The Cottage." Here my father and his siblings had also lived when they were younger.

The inside of the house was dark and the furniture black, brown and green. Heavy draperies shut out the daylight from the windows. The only sound breaking the silence was the ticking and bonging of the many wall clocks and cuckoo clocks in every room of the house. Mutti's father had been a watchmaker in Basel, Switzerland, and therefore she had all these clocks. Once, when Peter was visiting over a weekend, he couldn't sleep because of the noise from the clocks. He sprang out of bed in the middle of the night and stopped all the pendulums, so that the house became dead silent. Some of the clocks got damaged. The next morning when Mutti noticed this, she was furious.

In the parlor was a grand piano that nobody played, and many bookcases, although neither of the grandparents read very much. If Mutti read it was mostly books by Vicky Baum, an Austrian writer of Mutti's generation. Peter called them "trash novels" but I wasn't sure what that meant. Daddy mainly read the paper, especially the financial news.

Daddy had a private chauffeur named Mr. Andersson who picked him up in a black Mercedes every morning and drove him to the office. When I started first grade this car was also used to drop me off at school. I was the only child in Alingsås who came to school by car and it was very embarrassing. I used to ask Mr. Andersson to let me out a block before the school, so that the other children wouldn't see the car. Sometimes I was discovered anyway, and teased.

I was also teased about my name. As a child I was called Randi, a Norwegian name that sounded like "striped" in

Swedish. The kids laughed at me and called me "chequered" and "dotted." I hated the name Randi and was glad when a few years later I could change it to Rebecca.

Mutti and Daddy were old-fashioned people, fixed in the ways of central Europe in the early 1900s. This was fine when I was a baby, but they did not know how to handle an older child. They did not understand the lifestyle of the 1950s in Sweden. Mutti did not allow me to take swimming lessons or do other sports, because "it wasn't lady like." Subsequently I became the only child in my class who was unable to do any sports or gymnastics. This made me even more anxious and introverted than I already was.

Mutti had a good heart, but a choleric temper and often got terribly angry, for no apparent reason. Her face became dark red and she shouted with great force. I never understood what she was upset about or why. Her eruptions were frightening, and while they lasted I used to run to my room and hide.

One time I made the gross error of saying to my teacher that my grandparents were German. I was seven years old and not yet educated in geography, history or religion, neither in school nor at home. I did not know why the Weiss family had moved to Sweden. Since Mutti and Daddy spoke German, I assumed they were German, whatever that meant. (Mutti was actually Swiss and Daddy Austrian-Hungarian, but German was their mother tongue.) When Mutti found out that I had "labeled them as Germans" she nearly fainted. *"We are not German!"* she screamed, her face almost purple with rage. "How *could* you say we are German? What if I told someone *you* were *Chinese?"* I had no idea why it was bad to be German or Chinese, but this time I was too scared to even hide in my room. I bolted out of the house and ran without stopping for ten minutes until I reached the house of Mrs. Olsson. She was Mutti's cleaning lady and always kind to me. Sobbing, I told Mrs. Olsson what had happened, and asked if I could stay in her house. Mrs. Olsson seemed to understand the situation, and did some mediation with Mutti over the phone. Eventually Mutti cooled down and I could go back home.

My father's sister Irene and her family also lived in Alingsås. Irene was nice, but tyrannized by Mutti. When Irene visited us, Mutti would criticize her and speak to her harshly. I always wondered why Mutti was so hard on her, and why Irene never protested. Instead of defending herself she sat silently with her head down, as though she were ashamed, although she had done nothing wrong.

There were several live-in maids during the years I was there. They were imported from German-speaking countries so that Mutti could communicate with them. Because of Mutti's temper they didn't last long, and I often found them crying in their rooms.

Daddy was a kind and gentle person (although I later heard he was a tough businessman). He did not protest when Mutti had her fits, other than quietly remarking: "Frau, welch ein Temperament" (Woman, what a temperament). He and Mutti were extremely close. Daddy was the only person Mutti never yelled at, and they never had any fights with each other. They were a unit and almost seemed like one person, in spite of their vast differences. Mutti was intense and dramatic, Daddy just the opposite. He didn't talk much, especially not about his background or family in Hungary and Austria, and he never mentioned that he was Jewish. The only hint of this was at bedtime, when Mutti and Daddy always sat by my bed for a while. Mutti, who was Catholic, used to make the sign of the cross and recite "Notre Père" (The Lord's Prayer) in French, which was her second language. Daddy never made the sign, and did not participate in the prayers. Later I understood that this had something to do with his religion.

Mutti and Daddy said they loved me, and I know they really did. I loved them too, especially Daddy, but they were so overprotective and humorless that I felt stifled and oppressed in their home. I cannot recall a single time when either of them laughed. At the most they would smile sadly. They had probably been like that ever since 1934, when their twelve-year-old daughter Margit was killed in a car accident. Daddy sometimes used to call me Margitlein because I had blue eyes like Margit and apparently resembled her.

Many years later I heard from Irene that Daddy on one single occasion had demonstrated some of his Jewish background. This was when Margit had died, and Daddy, in deepest despair, sat by her coffin. He was rocking back and forth and reciting the Kaddish, the Hebrew Prayer for the Dead. Irene wondered what the strange language was, but didn't dare to ask.

This time, like the time before, I stayed two years with my grandparents. When I was nine, Helga decided to take me back, and I returned to Stockholm. Mutti and Daddy wept when I left. It was the second time I was torn away from them, and I think it broke their hearts. Although I had not been happy in their home, I felt bad about leaving them.

In the 1980s I had a one-woman show at the Alingsås Fine Art Museum. It was the first time I had been back in Alingsås since Mutti and Daddy died in 1959. It was a bittersweet experience—recalling both my love for these two beings, and my difficult years with them. I went to look at the big brown villa, which seemed smaller now. Strangers were living there, but they invited me in.

I stayed with my aunt Irene, who had never moved from Alingsås. She was chronically ill and had a tragic life, but was still a warm and caring person. Before she became ill she had been a highly esteemed teacher of dance and music. She wrote a book about her life called *Auf der Suche nach einer Heimat* (In search of a homeland), published in German in 2001.

It was good to meet a couple of old school friends who

came to the opening of the exhibition. Even Liesbeth, one of the maids Mutti had abused, showed up. She had married a Swede and stayed in Alingsås.

I often think about Mutti and Daddy. I wish I had understood them better and shown them more appreciation while they were alive. I wish I had insisted on learning more about their life in Germany, their background and families. Now Peter, Irene and Alexander are also gone, and there is no one left to ask.

EMMA

In the summers I usually stayed with Peter. One or another of his many mistresses was always present, often with their own children.

One summer in the early 1950s Peter and I traveled to a small town in southern Sweden, where he had rented a cottage together with some fellow artists. There he had a girlfriend named Emma. She had brown hair, a radiant face, and was always cheerful and friendly. Emma used to hug me and talk to me. She was interested in *me*, not just in Peter, and that made me very happy. Emma was much nicer than my own mother, who was seldom around and who seemed absent-minded whenever she did spend time with me.

Near our house was a large heath covered with heather and flowers in many colors. Emma and I used to walk there in the white summer nights, just the two of us. She talked about her own childhood, recited poetry, and told jokes that made me laugh. Those were joyful moments.

Emma was good at sewing and took the time to make a dress for me. It was white with a pattern of pink and red roses and I wore it with pride. "Emma made this dress for me," I told everybody.

I was given a little book with blank pages, a "poetry

album," which many Swedish children used to have. Peter, Emma and the other artists made drawings and wrote poems in it and the book became a treasure that I saved all my life. Peter made a portrait of himself sitting in the garden, smiling. He also wrote a long poem, but it wasn't very good. Making rhymes in Swedish was not his forte.

One morning I asked Peter as usual: "Where is Emma?" "Emma has gone back to her husband," Peter answered calmly. This was very confusing. Emma had a husband? I was grief-stricken, but Peter gave no explanation. Apparently it was entirely normal that a married woman had been living with him and then suddenly disappeared.

I didn't see Emma again until 1982 when Peter's sudden death was reported on TV and in the newspapers. Shortly after his funeral we somehow got in touch and had lunch together in a restaurant. Emma, who was now in her fifties, told me she had been madly in love with Peter but that her husband never knew about their liaison. Emma had been shocked when she heard on TV about Peter's death. Her daughters had been with her when she watched the evening news, and since they knew nothing, she had to hide her shock and her tears. It had been very difficult for her.

For some reason I didn't ask Emma why she had left me without explanation when I was a child. I think I was embarrassed to tell her how much she had meant to me. And now, as an adult, I could well imagine what might have transpired between her and Peter. They probably quarreled in the evening when I was asleep, and Emma ran away in tears or in anger. Perhaps she was hoping that Peter would beg her to return, and when he didn't, she stayed with her husband. Or maybe she realized that Peter was not a reliable partner, and that her husband was a better man. Still, she could have said good-bye to me.

THE WALDORF SCHOOL

When I was about to start third grade, Helga began to understand that she had a daughter she was responsible for. I don't know what brought about this realization, but something must have happened in her life. She took me to Stockholm, where I lived with her until I was fifteen. These were rough years for both of us, for our relationship was damaged beyond repair. Irrationally, I blamed Helga more than Peter for having abandoned me for so many years. I had no love, trust or respect for her, and took revenge by disturbing her artistic work and being as mean, disobedient and troublesome as possible. I refused to speak to her boyfriends, and made a scene whenever she went to her studio. It was surprising that she accepted it and didn't send me away again. But Helga had started her long "recompense," which she continued to the end of her life.

I was put in a Waldorf school for five years. Its educational system was based on Anthroposophy, the philosophy of Rudolf Steiner, the Austrian scientist who lived in the late 1800s and early 1900s. The classes were small and we stayed with the same main teacher until we were fourteen years old. My teacher, Miss Lundmark, was a devoted Anthroposophist and a passionate but stern educator. I found her intimidating, but she cared a great deal about her students and was interested in each one of us.

As a private school, receiving no financial support from the Swedish government, it depended completely on private donations. The parents paid what they could afford—the wealthy ones (of whom there were just a few) paid more, and the poor ones paid less. Only a small percentage of the parents were Anthroposophists, but they liked the school anyway, as it was considered a humane and high-quality institution.

It was housed in an old, dilapidated building in the center of Stockholm. In those days the staff had no money for renovations. Decades later they built their own school, very aesthetic with its own special architecture.

I didn't understand much about Anthroposophy, but was told it was a science of the spirit. It seemed to be partly Christian, partly Hindu or Buddhist. The Anthroposophists believed in reincarnation and it was said that some of the teachers remembered their past lives.

Instead of buying schoolbooks, we made and illustrated our own, based on the information Miss Lundmark gave us. I especially enjoyed creating my own history books with colorful drawings of ancient Pharaohs and Roman senators. There was strong emphasis on the arts. We played the flute and sang in choirs, but in the painting classes we were only allowed to use certain "harmonious" colors and no other. We also did "eurythmy"—some kind of rhythmic movements with rods. None of the students liked the eurythmy classes and we sighed and groaned when it was time for them.

Moral rules were very strict. Sex was never discussed. Some foods, like chocolate, were forbidden. Movies and pop music were frowned upon, but we secretly listened to Elvis Presley and danced rock 'n' roll.

There was also a certain Anthroposophic dress code, quite attractive with its hand-dyed flowing cottons, but those who dressed differently (like me) were despised.

When the girls in my class were about thirteen we began

to use a tiny bit of make-up. I will never forget when Miss Lundmark discovered that one of the girls had painted her lips. The girl received a slap in the face and was sent to the bathroom to wash off the lipstick.

During my first years at the Waldorf school I was bullied because I was tall, skinny, pale and shy. The children from Anthroposophist families were often the worst bullies. They pulled my hair, beat me and called me the Ghost or the Skeleton. The bullying was traumatic for me. I so much wanted to be strong and self-confident like many other kids seemed to be, but I just wasn't. Instead of fighting back, I retreated into my shell, tried to make myself invisible and to show no emotions. But I was miserable and often came home from school crying. Helga talked to Miss Lundmark about it, and I assume Miss Lundmark talked to my tormentors, but it didn't have much effect.

On one occasion the roles were reversed and I suddenly became a tormentor myself. In our class there was a fat girl, who was also constantly bullied. One day I joined the others in heckling her. For once I was not the victim, and I was secretly elated, although I tried to act cool and bored. I still blush with shame when I think about it.

One morning in third grade I was standing alone in a corner of the school yard, teased and pushed around by a group of kids. A classmate named Suzanne Osten then came over to me, stood by my side and defended me against the bullies. That was very courageous of her, and it was how our friendship started. This friendship was one of the reasons the bullying eventually ended, and I became reasonably accepted and assimilated in the class. Suzanne and I remained best friends for years, and we still correspond.

In the 1980s I attended a class reunion in Stockholm.

Apart from Suzanne I hadn't seen any of the students since we were children. Now we were all around forty years old. Some of the students had wrinkles and paunches and were unrecognizable, some seemed not to have changed at all. It was a strange and touching reunion. The students sat around a large table, and each one related what they had been doing since they left the school. A couple of them openly admitted that they were alcoholics and social misfits. Others were active Anthroposophists who worked for the school, which had expanded and flourished since the 1950s. Many had enrolled their own children. I met some of my old tormentors who were now quite friendly and had conveniently forgotten what transpired between us as kids.

The fat girl was now thin as a stick, very pretty, and had become an accomplished actress. I asked her to forgive me for that time I bullied her, but she said she didn't remember it. That probably wasn't true. I believe these cruelties scar you for life and wish there were ways to prevent them from happening.

Miss Lundmark was also present, now in her sixties and still an ardent Anthroposophist. She told us about her life and said she had loved us, every child in the class.

The percentage of artists was high. Five out of our class of twenty were successful artists of various kinds. I think that speaks well for the Waldorf system.

As an adult I read some of Steiner's books and gained a better understanding of Anthroposophy. I admire their biodynamic farming, their holistic and homeopathic way of treating illness, and their spiritual view on life.

ALMUÑECAR

Almuñecar is a small coastal town in southern Spain. In the 1950s it was no more than a fishing village. That was before the tourists discovered Almuñecar and before there were luxury hotels and other attractions.

Most of the town consisted of simple stone cottages built along a mountain slope. The narrow streets abounded with dirty children and stray cats and dogs. It smelled of garbage, fish and olive oil. There was great poverty and many people were illiterate. Some lived in caves in the mountain. The few who had a bit of education or money lived in a small area of better homes down by the beach.

This was during the time of General Franco. There was political suppression, and the "Guardia Civil"—a fierce-looking police force—was patrolling every city and village.

In spite of this, there was a small Scandinavian artist colony in Almuñecar, and some of Helga's colleagues lived there. Helga wanted to go there and paint, and she took me along. It was the summer I turned eleven, and a happy time for a change.

When Helga and I lived in Stockholm we fought almost daily, but when we traveled our relationship always improved. We both put our attention outwards, savored the new impressions and adventures, and our internal problems diminished.

We found a small apartment with white-washed walls, heavy dark-brown furniture and uncomfortable, screeching beds. Salaries in southern Spain were so low that Helga could afford to hire a maid. Her name was Pepita; she was seventeen years old but no taller than me. She did our laundry on a washboard down by the sea, and was always singing "Maria de los remedios" in a loud and piercing voice.

I learned some elementary Spanish and played with Spanish children, who had peculiar names like Incarnacion and Consuelo. We rode on donkeys and made castles of sand on the beach.

The adults loved the Spanish food, especially paella, a yellowish dish with rice, shrimps and clams. But I thought clams were revolting and longed for Scandinavian pastries— the ones we bought in Almuñecar were made with olive oil and tasted awful.

One of the Swedish artists in Almuñecar was Bengt Eriksson, who was married to Evert Taube's daughter Ellinor. (Taube is the "national song writer" of Sweden and very famous there.) Bengt, nicknamed Benito, was a handsome man with curly blond hair and bright blue eyes. Apparently he had left his wife and was now living alone on a farm with their two-year-old daughter. Benito drank a lot of wine and was sometimes seen dead drunk riding on a donkey with his little daughter in front of him. In spite of his drinking he was kind and friendly, especially to children.

Benito used to imitate and make fun of the Guardia Civil behind their backs, scaring us all. It was well known that it could be dangerous to upset the Guardia. He also led the group on excursions to Flamenco clubs and bullfights in nearby cities like Malaga and Almeria. (Helga and I couldn't stand cruelty to animals and refused to go to the bullfights.)

Before Benito became an artist he had been a sailor and

had traveled all over the world. He had been in many terrible fights and his body was full of scars that he proudly showed us. He used to tell me hair-raising stories about his adventures. One time when he was in Africa, he had been attacked by four men in a dark tunnel, and had been forced to kill them all in self defense.

Another time Benito had been shipwrecked and was drifting in a life-boat for many days, with no food and almost no water. He was close to death when he was rescued by the crew of a fishing trawler. After he was pulled aboard the captain gave Benito half a cup of lukewarm cocoa. Later he got a few cookies, and the next day a small meal. Benito said the captain saved his life again by giving him only the cocoa when they found him. I was very impressed by Benito's stories. It didn't occur to me that they might not all be entirely true.

Among Helga's friends, Benito was my favorite. But I also liked the Danish artist Ingrid Vang Nyman, nicknamed Pus. She was a pale, ethereal and highly sensitive woman. Pus had made all the illustrations for Pippi Longstocking and most of Astrid Lindgren's books, and in my poetry album she made a stunning painting of a Japanese child.

That summer in Spain there were two fantastic experiences. The first was the encounter with Flamenco dance and music. I loved the Flamenco and couldn't get enough of it. The proud, fiery gypsy dancers, the exhilarating exotic music, the colorful dresses, laces and fans were fascinating. Pepita, who was an excellent seamstress, made a flamenco dress for me. It was white with blue dots, had many layers of ruffles and a white lace petticoat. I treasured this dress and never discarded it, even years after I had grown out of it and it was practically in shreds.

The other was the discovery of the Alhambra in the nearby city of Granada. Oh, what a palace! I had never seen anything so beautiful. This Islamic castle had been built by the Moors on the top of a mountain in the Middle Ages. Every inch of it was decorated with intricate ornaments and patterns in soft pastel colors. There were courtyards with fountains and sculptures of lions, marvelous rose gardens, exquisite landscaping and huge olive trees. I fantasized about the Moorish kings and veiled harem ladies who had lived there hundreds of years earlier.

As a special treat a photographer dressed me up as an Arab princess and took a picture of me by one of the lovely courtyards. That photo became another of my treasures.

There was great artistic inspiration in this trip to Spain, even for an eleven-year-old. For years my sketch-books were full of castles, harem girls and flamenco dancers.

Just as I had revisited Alingsås, I made a new trip to Almuñecar and Granada in the 1980s. Almuñecar was now a popular tourist resort and unrecognizable. Alhambra was unchanged and still magical in its timeless splendor.

COPENHAGEN

The summer I turned fifteen Peter took me on a trip to Copenhagen, the capital of Denmark. At this point we had quite a good relationship. Peter used to tell me about his youth in Germany, England, Czechoslovakia and Switzerland. He described the Academy of Art in Prague where he had been trained, paintings he did there, and the first books he wrote. I was always interested in these stories and could easily identify with a refugee like Peter. I also often felt like a stranger in Sweden and in Helga's aristocratic family, although I was born and raised in Stockholm. Sometimes I caught myself thinking: "Thank God I speak such good Swedish."

Peter and I talked about many things, but Skå was never mentioned. He knew what had happened there, but the subject was somehow taboo. With the strange resilience of children I had pushed Skå out of my mind, and my natural love for Peter had gradually returned.

A few months before our trip to Copenhagen, Mutti had died of a heart attack. Daddy, who could not live without Mutti, faded away and died too within another couple of months. It was sad, for both Peter and me. Peter later wrote a book which was partly about them, and which I read when it was published. It was a sinister novel with sentences stretching over half a page. I did not recognize Mutti and Daddy in Peter's book—they must have treated him quite differently than they treated me. They were hard on him and used corporal punishment, but on me they never laid a hand.

Peter had inherited Daddy's old black Mercedes, and with this car we were now going south. Peter was slow and awkward with the car and never drove faster than 30 miles per hour! He probably didn't have a driver's license. It took us a whole day to get to Småland, a hilly county in southern Sweden. There Peter visited one of his girlfriends, a redheaded actress whose name I don't remember. She was single with a toddler. It was obvious that she was in love with Peter, and she didn't talk to me at all. I wondered why all these women were so attracted to Peter. I suppose he could be sensitive and understanding, and I suppose he was handsome and exotic with his thick black hair, melancholy eyes, and a slight foreign accent. You couldn't really tell what the accent was—his native language was German but it wasn't really a German accent. He had lived in many countries, and was only twenty years old when he arrived in Sweden. In the years to come, even my girlfriends, who were my age, fell in love with him. I thought that was disgusting.

In Stockholm Peter normally lived with Gunilla, since a few years back, but apparently they were now on a break from each other. This saddened me, because I had become quite attached to Gunilla. She was blonde and pretty, twelve years younger than Peter and more like a sister or friend to me than a stepmother.

When we were on the road again, Peter wanted to hear my opinion of the actress. Did I think she could be a good substitute for Gunilla? No, I definitely did not think so.

Eventually we arrived in Copenhagen, where we stayed with Barbro, another of Peter's lovers. She was a film director, and had two daughters, aged fourteen and seventeen. All the women in that family were tall and good-looking, but Cleo, the oldest daughter, was particularly stunning. She had eyes the color of amber and long lashes and I couldn't stop staring at her.

Copenhagen, although in Scandinavia and only eight hours drive from Stockholm, (for those who drive at normal speed) had a continental flair. It was a livelier city than Stockholm and there was always something fun to do at night.

One evening we went to a jazz club. There Cleo caught the eye of the performing saxophonist, Stan Getz, and he invited us backstage. Soon he started a relationship with Cleo. I was enormously impressed and envious—no jazz musician had ever hit on me.

Peter seemed to be getting on well with Barbro, but after some time he wanted to go home. He told me he realized that he liked Gunilla better than any of the others, and we returned to Stockholm.

To my delight, Gunilla and Peter soon got back together. During the next few years Gunilla and I became very close. She was my best adult friend and I told her everything about myself. My relationship with Helga was still bad, and we seldom had any important conversations. Peter liked to talk about himself, but got impatient when he had to listen to *me* for more than a couple of minutes. Gunilla on the other hand could listen, and treated me as an adult even in my early teens. She confided in me and even discussed Peter's many infidelities, which were hard on her. I couldn't fathom how Peter could be so mean to Gunilla.

It was easy for me to identify with Gunilla, for she had also had a rough childhood, worse than mine in fact, and like me she was an unhappy person. We shared each other's pain and problems, but were also able to laugh and joke about them. Gunilla was a ceramist and set designer; we had the same type of cultural background, and many interests in common. I adored Gunilla.

Peter had abandoned me as a child, left me at Skå, and now I saw him hurt Gunilla as well. He also was not a good father to Paul, his son from a brief marriage in 1949, nor to Micke, Gunilla's son from a previous marriage. Peter was unpredictable, complex and selfish. Like Mutti he would sometimes frighten his family by getting terribly upset without apparent cause. Sometimes he was completely withdrawn for days and didn't talk to anybody, which also scared me.

Yet I loved my father. There was a kind of bond between us—somehow I understood him. He was lonely and homeless in spite of all his women, and I could understand this homelessness. My own personality was similar to his, for better or worse.

According to Helga and Gunilla, Peter was very fond of me. But he never said so to me, and although we talked a lot, he didn't show much physical affection. I wasn't sure how he really felt about me. I so much wanted him to love me, accept me and be proud of me. Instead of just being myself, I tried to be the way I thought he wanted me to be. I tried to voice opinions he would agree with, and tried to sound analytical and intellectual, like he sounded. This did not always work. Sometimes I gave the "wrong" answer and was embarrassed when he disagreed with "my" opinions.

Later in life I had many dreadful upsets and arguments with Peter, and it took a long time before I could forgive him for some of the cruel and unfair things he did. Even so, he had his good points.

All my life, from my earliest childhood, he encouraged and admired my artistic creations. He took me to many art exhibitions. The most outstanding was one of Anna Casparsson, an old woman who made magnificent fabric appliqués. She had constructed a world of dreams and fairy tales, in silk, velvet, beads and lace. I was only five years old, but seeing her work made me decide to make fiber art, and this has been my main medium ever since.

Gunilla, Peter and I often went to the movies, and saw films by great directors like Bergman, Kazan, Bunuel and Cassavetes. I was smuggled into the R-rated ones.

Peter had also started to make his own films, which were experimental and surrealistic. Sometimes I was present when he worked. One of his full-length movies was called *Mirage* and starred Gunilla and Staffan Lamm. It was interesting to watch the production, but when I saw the completed movie in the theatre I didn't really understand what it was about. I asked Peter, but his answer was vague.

Peter encouraged me to read good literature. He gave me books by Hermann Hesse and Luise Rinser, and told me about the summer of 1937 when he was staying with Hesse in Switzerland. His friendship with Hesse had been important for him and it was inspiring for me to hear about it. Peter showed me illustrations he had made for some of Hesse's short stories. I also held Hesse in high esteem and his books influenced me greatly. *Siddhartha* is still one of my favorite novels, as is *Rings of Glass* by Luise Rinser.

SUMMERHILL

In the beginning of 1960 I was sent to Summerhill School in England. The Steiner school had ended after eighth grade and then the students had to find other schools. It was very hard to fit into the normal educational system after five years in a Waldorf. I tried two or three public schools, but hated them. The classes were large, the teachers bored and careless. I refused to go back to them.

Peter had read the books of A.S. Neill, the founder and headmaster of Summerhill, and he liked Neill's ideas. So I was sent to England—my first trip abroad by myself. I was glad to leave Stockholm and my conflicts with Helga.

Summerhill is a boarding school situated near the small town of Leiston, on the east coast of England. It consisted of a large two-storey house surrounded by several smaller cottages. The kitchen, dining room, offices and assembly hall were on the ground floor of the large building, and the students' rooms were on the second floor. Each bedroom was shared by two or three children and there were a couple of old-fashioned bathrooms (with tubs only, no showers) that were shared by all. The classrooms were in the smaller, separate houses. Neill and his family, and the other teachers lived in their own cottages. The buildings were old, had no central heating and were freezing in the winter. Gravel roads, meadows and fields surrounded the school.

At that time there were only twenty-seven pupils, aged five to sixteen. Many were around fifteen like me. Some of them had been "problem children" who could not adjust in their previous schools. (After spending some time at Summerhill, they usually ceased being problem children.) Others were "normal" kids who were there because their parents endorsed Neill's philosophy.

There were five teachers, including Neill himself, and a couple of housemothers. The teachers and adults were called by their first names—not Sir or Miss like in other schools. Neill, then in his late seventies, was still bright and active as an instructor and headmaster. Everyone called him Neill, as though that were his first name. He was tall, had white hair, wore old corduroy pants and wrinkled jackets, and usually smoked a pipe. His dog followed him everywhere.

The school was unique because we had self-government and total democracy. Every Saturday night there was a mandatory meeting where things were discussed, planned, voted on and decided. Each child and adult had one vote. Complaints were brought up, and some kids were fined part of their pocket money and told to repair or otherwise take responsibility for any damage they might have caused. No other actions were taken, as Neill did not believe in punishment.

It was unique also because children didn't have to go to classes if they didn't want to. Neill was against enforced education. Normally, when a new student arrived, he (or she) was thrilled with the new freedom and didn't go to a single class the first days or weeks. But soon he would get bored, and would voluntarily go to classes. Because it was now his free will, learning would be easier and results better. Such was the theory, anyway. Most of the kids did go to classes, and most of them passed their exams.

I skipped school the first week. Then I enrolled in Neill's

classes of English Grammar and Literature. I also took other subjects, such as German, French, and Art, but was glad I didn't have to take Physics and Chemistry, which were my weak areas. In the Literature class Neill gave us interesting writing assignments, like "write a biography about yourself, as though you are now an old person and someone else is describing the life you have lived." I wrote about a life in Israel and America, even though I had never had any contact with those two countries at that point in my life. Although I had two Jewish grandparents—Peter's father and Helga's mother—I was not brought up Jewish, and Israel was never mentioned. (Later, I did indeed end up in both Israel and America.)

As far as I recall, there were no gym classes or organized sports being taught at Summerhill. But every night there was music in the assembly hall, and most of us danced rock 'n' roll. There were enough bicycles to go around, and we used them all the time. Some kids played tennis or football, and in the summer we went to the beach to swim. Nobody was taunted for not participating. All the physical activities were spontaneous and initiated by the children, not by the teachers. For me it was a tremendous relief to not be forced to do sports. This way I could choose my own activities and could gradually learn games like table tennis which I eventually became quite good at.

On Tuesday nights Neill would gather the kids and make up stories in which we were all involved. One story was about a ship on the high seas, where all of us were sailors. Neill invented all kinds of adventures happening to us, and asked us to contribute to the story. Each child, in turn, created a new chapter.

The general atmosphere at Summerhill was relaxed and tolerant. The adults were not stern and rigid like many of the teachers in the Waldorf school. I never saw a child being bullied and was not bullied myself. The older children treated the younger ones in a remarkably tender and caring way. Since we were not oppressed and abused by our teachers or the system, we were less inclined to abuse each other.

Sometimes we talked to Neill about religion and asked his opinion of Jesus. Neill said that every child was basically like Jesus and that no religion was needed. I thought about that for long time. Was it possible that I too was fundamentally good, although I had so many faults?

The "PLs"—private lessons—were famous at Summerhill. These were not actually lessons, but more like psychotherapy that Neill gave to students who wanted them. I didn't like the PLs. I thought Neill's questions were silly, and I had already been analyzed to death by various practitioners my parents had sent me to as a child. After the first PL I avoided them carefully.

Neill did not believe in preventing teenagers from having a love life. He did not encourage it, but did not try to suppress it. Among the students were a girl and a boy who were in love and wanted to be together. Instead of condemning their relationship, Ena, Neill's wife, took the girl to a doctor where she was fitted with a diaphragm.

There were no locks on the bathroom doors anywhere in the building. (Only the toilets had locks.) Since I was a shy and inhibited person I did not take a bath for the first two weeks, terrified that some boy would walk in when I was in the bathtub. Finally I got so dirty that I was forced to take a bath. I tried to pick a time of day when the boys were unlikely to be around, and one afternoon I was in the bathtub, hoping for the best. To my horror the door opened and one of the sixteen-year-old boys walked in. He washed his hands in the sink, and carried on a casual conversation with me, paying no attention to the fact that I was naked. I was too embarrassed to speak. Then he walked out as casually as he had walked in. This incident made me less timid, and I was no longer afraid to take baths.

I soon realized that the kids in this school never made a

big deal about nakedness. They didn't giggle or make "dirty jokes" and had no obsessive interest in sex.

The teachers at Summerhill were idealistic and unconventional. As the school had constant financial problems, they got paid very little, but they weren't there for the money. Ulla, who taught German, French and Sewing, and Harry, the Art teacher, were both Germans who had immigrated to England in the 1930s, because they disagreed with the Nazis. Another teacher, an Englishman, was fired when a sixteen-year-old boy from Leiston was found in his bed.

People came from near and far to visit Summerhill. One of them was an Israeli singer, Nechama Haendel, who stayed a few days and sang for us. I was mesmerized by her beautiful songs. They struck a chord in me that I could not explain, a chord that kept vibrating long after Nechama left. Something about the Hebrew language and the stories she told us about Israel touched me profoundly.

I spent almost a year at Summerhill. I learned to speak English, and it was an overall therapeutic time. Some of my awkwardness and insecurity faded away. I also noticed that boys liked me, which was a surprising and novel experience. Apparently I wasn't quite as ugly and repulsive as I had previously thought.

After Neill's death in 1973, Ena ran the school. Later their daughter Zoe took over and is still the headmistress. I get occasional email from her, and from other Summerhill friends.

I am glad I had the opportunity to go to a Waldorf school as well as a free school like Summerhill. Both of them are among the best educational systems in the world—especially for human, artistic and spiritual growth. Here I have to thank both Peter and Helga who were willing to pay for these relatively expensive private schools.

LONDON

Most kids at Summerhill took their exams and left the school when they were around sixteen. When I was sixteen and a half I felt I should also move on. I wasn't sure where to go, but did not want to return to Sweden. With some difficulty I got my parents' permission (and financial support) to study art in London, and that is where I moved in January 1961.

My new home was a rented room in Hampstead, a district where many artists lived. Five days a week I took the double-decker bus to the art school which was near Notting Hill, another London district. I got basic training in life-drawing, painting, sculpture, stained glass and art history. The school had an inexpensive cafeteria, where I used to have lunch with the other students. Apart from that I didn't eat much, because I had never learned to cook, and though I was 5'10", I only weighed 118 pounds.

On the weekends I was involved in the Campaign for Nuclear Disarmament (CND), and took part in many demonstrations against the bomb. During one sit-in, about a hundred of us were brutally dragged away by the police, and taken to jail. It was quite a scary experience. Luckily the CND organizers paid my fine and bailed me out.

In London I had my first boyfriend, a young actor named Michael Gothard. We met at a CND demonstration. He was tall, blond, handsome and gifted. I was dazzled and flattered that he liked me, and spent every weekend with him. But he was just as neurotic as I was, and we tortured each other emotionally. Michael had a cruel streak, and our relationship destabilized me. I was far from ready to live with a man, and especially not with him.

Life in London seemed hazy and unreal. I felt like a leaf blowing in the wind, and suffered from dark depressions. I did not know how to live or how to be happy. I had never known any rules, never seen examples or standards of how to live a sane life. I did not know what would help me or what would hurt me, and I made many errors.

Peter and Helga had not been happy, neither together nor by themselves. They were frantically hunting for fulfillment by having affairs and by traveling. When I was about thirteen Peter encouraged me to start having sexual relationships. He said it was natural to experiment, and good for artists. But I was very shy, and before Michael I had never even been kissed.

Mutti and Daddy did not give me any guidelines. They only conveyed a vague feeling that life was difficult and that it was best not to talk about it.

Helga's parents, whom I had also sometimes lived with as a child, did not teach me anything. Helga's mother Signe was sweet but irresponsible and out of touch with modern life. Helga's father, a prominent professor at the Karolinska Institute (and divorced from Signe), talked only about science and was incapable of discussing anything personal or emotional.

The psychologists I had been to certainly did not help me either. Many children of Swedish artists and intellectuals were sent to psychotherapists. But all I really would have needed was a stable adult who loved me and gave me some sane and basic rules to live by—like "do not lie, do not hurt others, do not be promiscuous, find a purpose in life and follow it." A few rules like that would have been worth a hundred hours of therapy. But not even Neill gave advice.

I wrote desperate letters to Suzanne Osten, who was still my best friend, and she wrote desperate letters back. We shared everything we couldn't tell the adults. It was good to be able to tell *someone*, and to know I wasn't the only one suffering. Suzanne's situation was in fact worse than mine, but somehow she kept her nose above the water.

When the spring semester ended I went back to Sweden. My affair with Michael was over. I wasn't sure what to do, and for lack of other ideas I applied to the College of Arts and Crafts in Stockholm. I was accepted and started my training there in the autumn.

Michael became a well-known actor in TV and movies, but sadly committed suicide in the 1990s. Suzanne, on the other hand, was able to overcome her unhappy childhood, and became a highly successful director of film and theatre.

ISRAEL

Nechama Haendel, the Israeli singer, was the first person who had made me aware of Israel. In 1961, when I was walking from London to Aldermaston in a mammoth march for nuclear disarmament, I briefly met a few more Israelis. They were the delegates of their country for this big demonstration, and the meeting with them struck that strange chord in me, once again. I knew I *had* to go to Israel.

In 1962, when I was not yet eighteen years old, I set out to Israel with my cousin Veronica. She was four years older than me, and a good friend. We went by train through Germany, Yugoslavia and Greece, and then by ship from Athens to Haifa. When we came ashore in Israel I was overcome with emotion and actually wept with joy. In some inexplicable way I felt I had come home.

How could I feel this way? Even my two Jewish grandparents had abandoned Judaism. Helga's mother came from a highly assimilated Swedish-Jewish family and did not think of herself as Jewish. Helga, whose father was Protestant, considered herself a Christian. Peter's father Eugen (Daddy) suppressed his Jewishness, and Peter was not raised as a Jew. Yet *I* felt so strongly about Israel. Was it the genes of my ancestors that spoke to me, or had I been Jewish in a past life?

Veronica and I had planned to spend two weeks in Israel. We saw the sights and did the usual tourist things. But when it was time to return to Sweden, I could not leave. Some powerful force made me stay put when Veronica went home. I managed to get a leave from my art school in Stockholm, and to get my parents' agreement. Peter was ambivalent regarding Israel. Because of his background he had a personal connection to the country, but he disagreed with its politics. Still, he didn't mind me staying in Israel, and gave me addresses of people he knew in Tel Aviv.

Through the Jewish Agency I came to a kibbutz which had an "Ulpan"—a Hebrew School—and a special department for new immigrants and foreign volunteers. The kibbutz was called Givat Chaim, which means Hill of Life. It was half-way between Tel Aviv and Haifa, near the small town of Hadera. Founded in the 1930s by immigrants from Germany, it had grown to nearly a thousand members. Some were concentration camp survivors who had arrived after the war.

Givat Chaim consisted of hundreds of small white cottages and bungalows. Every married couple, or single older person, had their own cottage. It had a bedroom, a bathroom, a kitchenette, and a small living room equipped with a radio and record player but no TV. The children lived by themselves in their own buildings, and unmarried youth lived in simple barracks, two persons to a room. In the center of the kibbutz was "Chaddar Ochel," the large communal dining hall where most people had their meals.

The kibbutz was a collective, self-supporting farming village. Surplus of food and other commodities were sold to outside villages or cities, and the revenue went into the general funds of the kibbutz. The members all worked eight hours a day but got no salaries, only pocket money. In the kibbutz store you could pick up free clothing, soap, towels, etc., and everyone got what they needed. On the counter was a basket with chocolate bars, cigarettes and condoms!

I joined a group of about twenty young people, all foreigners like myself. We were housed in barracks on the outskirts of the kibbutz. Some were Jewish, some not. Some were preparing their aliyah (immigration), some were more or less on holiday. They came from many European countries and from America, Australia and Africa. We were all given Hebrew names, and I was now called Rivka.

Among the people I befriended in this group were two Swedish-Jewish girls named Tana Ross (then Meyer) and Channa Bankier. They were close to me for years and are still my friends. Tana was a Holocaust survivor who had come to Sweden as a small child after the war. In spite of her background she was enthusiastic and vivacious. After Israel she moved to New York where she became an excellent documentary film producer. Channa's parents had miraculously escaped from the Warsaw Ghetto and come to Sweden, where Channa was born after the war. Channa later became a famous and controversial artist.

We worked about four hours a day, in all the different areas of the kibbutz. Those who were assigned to the fields often started their working day at 6:00 a.m. as it was too hot to work there later in the day. At 5:00 a.m., when it was still dark and cold outside, we gathered in the dining hall. There we were served hot tea and the standard kibbutz breakfast of boiled eggs, tomatoes, cucumber, newly baked bread and a kind of yoghurt called "lebben." Everything was fresh and produced in the kibbutz and I had never before tasted such delicious eggs and vegetables. After the meal we climbed into open trucks and went out to the fields, where we picked oranges, peaches or avocados. It was dawn when we arrived, but soon the sun came up. In the summer it was boiling hot at 10:00 a.m. and we were glad our working day was over.

Some of us milked the cows in the barn, tended to the turkeys, washed dishes in the giant collective kitchen, or served food in the dining hall. Some worked in the medical clinic, in the tailor's shop, or in the small factory that produced jam and canned fruit. All jobs had equal status, and we rotated between them. In return we received room and board, pocket money and Hebrew lessons.

It was good for me to do physical work for the first time in my life. I learned some discipline and how to function in a group. In the beginning this was tough—nobody had demanded much from me so far in my life. But now I was part of a group and my contribution was expected and needed. I rebelled against it but liked it at the same time.

I soon noticed that in the kibbutz you were judged solely on your performance as a worker. If you worked diligently and turned out good products you were liked and admired. If you were lazy, your co-workers despised you—you could tell from the way they treated the sluggards. This attitude and philosophy was new to me, and I tried to work hard. My pride and self-respect soared when I did a good job and got a pat on the back from a kibbutz member.

In the afternoons we studied the new language. It was difficult for many, especially for the English and American students, but was surprisingly easy for me. I loved the Israeli folksongs and dances and was elated when I moved to the music. Folk dancing was a delightful group activity, almost spiritual, not like dancing with boys at parties or in clubs, which I hated. For the rest of my life I would be looking for Israeli folk dance groups, and would find them all over the world.

From Friday afternoon to Sunday morning we were free, and spent the weekends hitch-hiking around the country.

Israel is so small that you can reach any point in the state within a few hours by car, no matter where you are located. I usually traveled with one or more of the other students, and we went everywhere—from Eilat to Nahariya, from Jerusalem to Yaffa.

Ein Gedi, up in the mountains above the Dead Sea, was a paradise. There were caves and caverns, myriads of sparkling waterfalls, and deep cool springs with the clearest water I had ever seen. Beautiful flora surrounded the wells. Wild antelopes roamed freely on the rocks, and uncommon birds were singing.

The Dead Sea is the lowest place on the planet—1286 feet below sea level. Its water was unbelievably salty and felt like oil, and we floated in it like balloons.

Lake Kinneret in the Galilee was also enthralling. There was something special and enigmatic about the Galilee. Thousands of years of religious history were still palpable in the town of Tiberias and the ancient villages around the lake.

Sometimes I visited Arje Griegst, a Danish goldsmith who was a guest teacher at the Bezalel Art School in Jerusalem. His apartment was close to the Arabic part of the city, which was blocked off with barbed wire. From Arje's roof terrace we could look down on houses and gardens on both the Israeli and Jordanian sides. One of these gardens was particularly splendid and mysterious with cypresses, orchids, live peacocks, ornamented gates and sculptures of stone. Arje and I sat on the terrace for hours, inventing stories about hidden treasures and secret rendezvous in this garden.

Other times I went with Channa to her parents who had a house in Herzlia. I envied Channa and wished I also had relatives in Israel. The Weiss family (earlier spelt Weisz) had scattered into Sweden, England and the USA when they had to flee from the Nazis in the 1930s. My grandfather Eugen

(Daddy) ended up in Sweden with his family. His sister Aranka went to England, and his brother Edmund to the U.S. None of them went to Israel. The other sister, Malvine, stayed in Austria and was killed by the Nazis. Helga's mother also had no relatives in Israel.

On our weekend trips we slept under trees or in youth hostels or in the homes of people we met on the road. I was seldom frightened, and seldom had any bad experiences. Hitch-hiking was the normal way of getting around. No car would ever pass without stopping to pick up hitch-hikers. They picked up everybody, men and women, young and old. In those days in Israel there was a definite feeling of belonging to one large family. Everyone seemed to care about everyone else.

When most of the other foreign students left Givat Chaim, I stayed. I became an assistant "metapelet"—a housemother in "Kita Dalet." This was the house of the children in fourth grade. I cherished the kids and did my best to be a good housemother although I was only eighteen myself.

In the kibbutzim ("im" is the plural ending of the word) children did not live with their parents, but in their own houses with their classmates. Here they ate, slept, played and studied with their teachers and housemothers. They visited their parents in the evenings and on the Sabbath. The parents helped the children with their homework and they sat together at dinner in the dining hall. Since the parents had no other responsibilities or financial worries after work, (and since there was no TV...) they were able to spend some quality time with their children.

Living apart seemed like a good idea to me. I thought there would be less tension and problems between parents and kids this way. The children seemed strong, stable and independent.

I had befriended two Givat Chaim families—the Fenigers and the Levys—spending much time with both the parents and their children who were my age. The parents captivated me. For hours I listened to stories of how they had arrived in Palestine, where they had come from, and what they had done before. What it was like during the British Mandate, and how they felt when Israel became a state.

Yitzchak Feniger had come from Vienna in the 1930s. His wife Aviva was a fifth generation sabra (born in Israel) from the ancient town of Tsfat. This was high status and very impressive. She was an abstract painter but had to do farm work like everyone else, so she painted in the evenings and weekends.

Ruth Levy had been a medical student in Germany until she was forced to leave. She was astute and energetic and made witty comments about everything. Her husband Aaron came from Strasbourg where he had been an engineer.

I also spent long evenings with other older kibbutz members. Many of them had been artists, writers, scientists and intellectuals before they came to the new country. They had joined the kibbutz because they were socialists and idealists. Palestine in the early days needed farmers and workers, not intellectuals. These people had willingly sacrificed their professions in order to build the new state. In the evenings I often found them in the collective library, reading and listening to classical music. They were like no other farmers anywhere in the world.

Some evenings I spent with concentration camp survivors. They were usually unwilling to discuss their experiences, but when they realized I was truly interested, they would sometimes talk a little. Their stories were horrifying and unfathomable, but somehow very real for me. It was as though the Holocaust had happened to me personally. I felt tremendous compassion for these beings who had been so destroyed. Every time I saw a tattooed number on an arm, my heart ached. It was clear to me that many of the survivors would never have a happy moment again, as long as they lived. Those who had died seemed to be the "lucky" ones. The survivors lived through the trauma every day for the rest of their lives.

I could see that coming to Israel had been a good choice for them. In the late 1940s, and even later, people in Europe and America did not know enough about the Holocaust. They did not understand the survivors and could not help them. The survivors were told to "forget" their suffering and not talk about it. But in Israel there were many others with similar experiences, and the survivors were respected and understood. Above all, in Israel there were new, glorious goals to work towards, and the survivors were needed to create the state.

Even in the 1960s, when I was there, anyone could perceive the joy and pride in building the Jewish nation. Especially the kibbutz was a fantastic place to be. Only a small percentage of Israel's population lived on kibbutzim, but they had a strong influence on the whole country. They were the most dedicated and unselfish people in Israel.

I admired the children and teenagers I got to know. They were often shy and quiet but seemed proud, straight and honorable. All were strong, hard-working, and good in sports. Girls as well as boys joined the army when they were eighteen and served two or three years. Every one of them was willing to die for Israel, and some of them did. I didn't have a single friend in Sweden who would voluntarily die for his country. On the contrary, the boys I knew there did everything in their power to avoid military service. In Israel the army was a normal part of life.

The children of each class stuck together and were each other's closest friends. They did not drink or take drugs and they were not promiscuous. Sometimes they had one or two relationships before they got married, but these would be long and serious.

It was next to impossible for a foreigner like me to penetrate that kind of group and become accepted by its members. It might have worked if I had become an immigrant and joined the army. In many ways I longed to do just that, but I was too young and insecure. I would have needed at least one close family member in Israel, like a parent or an aunt, someone I had known all my life. The idea of joining the army was unsettling. It was too different from the life I had lived in Europe.

However, it was very possible to create friendships with single individuals. Amnon Levy, who was a year older than me, became a close friend. He was a gifted artist who planned to become an architect. I was very fond of him and his mother, Ruth, and younger brother Rani, who was painfully shy. When I re-visited Israel in the 1970s I got to know Rani better. By then he was married to Tova, who also became a friend. She was training to be a diplomat for Israel and later served in many countries.

The Levys kept in touch with me for decades, and stayed with me in Sweden and France. As the years went by, I came to consider them almost as part of my own family.

Ofer Feniger, the son of Yitzchak and Aviva, was equally close to me. He was killed in Jerusalem in the six-day war of 1967, when he was only twenty-four years old. We had been corresponding, and it was a terrible shock when I heard of his death. He was an artist as well as an athlete and paratrooper, and a star of a person. It was my first real encounter with death, and it became a turning point in my life.

Before leaving Israel I spent a few months in Tel Aviv, where I shared an apartment with Shosh Morris, a kind and lovely English girl who had been my roommate in the kibbutz as well.

Somehow I landed a job as an assistant stage designer at the Habima, Israel's national theatre. There I made friends with the actors, playwrights and designers, like Helen Oxenbury, who was very talented and later became a writer and illustrator of children's books. (We lost contact when I left Israel, but reconnected in 2003.)

I also befriended a few Palestinians, like the poet Rashid Hussein, and for the first time I heard their side of the story. Life in Israel was hard for them. They did not feel accepted and were often bitter and unhappy.

Between the jobs in the theatre I was as usual traveling around the country. One weekend I took the bus down to Beer Sheva in southern Israel to meet an American film team that was going to make a movie about Moses. I was one of the many local extras they had employed, and was supposed to stay with them in their hotel. I arrived in Beer Sheva late on a Friday afternoon. There I found out that the producer had changed his mind and decided it was cheaper to make the movie in Hollywood! The crew had scattered during the day and left Beer Sheva.

It was almost dark outside and the buses had stopped going, so I couldn't leave town. To hitch-hike by myself at night was too risky. I was alone in an unfamiliar city with no friends or money for a hotel. It was getting cold and I shivered in my shorts and thin jacket. For hours I walked the streets aimlessly, looking in vain for someone I knew from the film team. Beer Sheva was an ancient, poor city in the middle of the desert, full of Bedouins and camels, veiled women and Moroccan immigrants. Swarthy, sweat-smelling men whispered to me in French and tried to pull me into doorways. I saw a couple of orthodox Jews and asked them for help, but they withdrew from me as though I were a leper. I didn't know then that the orthodox would never speak to a girl with bare legs.

About 10:00 p.m., when I was close to panic, I happened to pass the only night club in Beer Sheva, fittingly named "The Last Chance." I stepped inside. It was a small club for students and hippies of various nationalities and here I found other young people to talk to. The owner of the club offered to let me sleep on the floor in the club, since I had nowhere to go, and so I did. The next day I hitch-hiked back to Tel Aviv with Matti, a boy I had met at the club.

How did I dare to make this trip by myself? How did I manage to sleep on the floor? How did I avoid getting raped or murdered in Beer Sheva? How could I feel so safe in Israel? Later it was hard to grasp.

Ohra Mandelbaum was a young writer whose first novel was published when she was only twenty years old. An actor at the Habima had introduced me to her. Ohra was the most intelligent and charismatic girl I had ever met, and the friendship with her turned my time in Tel Aviv into magic. Throughout the spring of 1963 I walked to her apartment almost every evening. She lived a few blocks from me, near the beach, and these walks are etched in my memory. The fruit trees on the boulevard were blooming, the twilight air was soft, and the waves gently rushing.

Ohra was slim, pretty, looked almost like a boy, and everyone was drawn to her. She had unique opinions on any subject and had a wisdom and perceptiveness that young people seldom have. I was thrilled and amazed that she wanted to befriend me. I couldn't understand what she saw in me, but it must have been something, for we kept in touch for many years.

She gave me a book of poems she had published. Although I now spoke fluent Hebrew, reading and writing was still very hard. But I read Ohra's poems so many times that I eventually knew them by heart.

During this time the trial of Adolf Eichmann was in progress in Jerusalem and everybody talked about it. In my discussions with Ohra, I naively repeated opinions I had heard from others or read in the paper: that Eichmann alone was responsible for the murder of thousands, that he was a monster who deserved to be executed. Ohra made me see that Eichmann was one of many cogwheels in a large machine and that most people in Germany and other countries, through their indifference, passivity or outright evil had contributed to making the Holocaust possible.

Tel Aviv was a large and international city. People there were usually not of the same ethical and moral caliber as the people in Givat Chaim. In the theatre and art circles life was wild, just like in other big cities. I didn't feel as safe in Tel Aviv as in the kibbutz, and only Ohra made me stay as long as I did.

Of all places on this planet, Israel is closest to my heart. It is the most enchanting of countries and has the most intriguing inhabitants. In spite of war and terrorism I often long to go back, and dream of peace between Israel and the Arabs.

In Florida, in the spring of 2003, I had the fortune to meet and listen to Zeinab Habash, the Secretary General of the Palestinian Ministry of Education. She was quietly working with a group of Israelis and Americans to create peace in the Middle East. It was extraordinary to see these enthusiastic and dedicated Palestinians and Israelis together. Not since 1977, when I saw Golda Meir and Anwar Sadat chat on TV, had I felt such hope that peace may be possible.

BACK TO EUROPE

Since I didn't have the courage to become an Israeli citizen, I might as well go back to Sweden. Ohra would also be leaving soon; she had received a scholarship to Cambridge University in England. In the summer of 1963, my roommate Shosh and I decided to return to Europe together.

On the boat from Haifa I already regretted leaving Israel, and wrote a nostalgic letter to Ofer Feniger. Little did I then know that I would never see him again.

The boat went to Naples, Italy, where Shosh and I stayed a day, pursued by lovesick Italians. Then we hitch-hiked to Paris. How we dared to jump into any car that stopped for us is once again incredible, but we managed surprisingly well.

From Paris, Shosh went to London, but I found a cheap hotel near Boulevard Saint Germain, and started to explore the surroundings. By chance I met two African-American girls, Brenda Dixon and Greer Johnson. Brenda was only two years older than me but already a professional ballet dancer, and Greer was training to be a teacher. The three of us became instant friends and went on excursions together. We climbed the Eiffel Tower, visited Notre Dame, and talked for hours in the outdoor cafés on the Left Bank. This was my first encounter with black Americans and I was horrified to hear about their lives in the U.S. I could easily understand what it was like to be oppressed and humiliated. I had read books by Richard Wright and James Baldwin, but it was different to hear these personal stories.

Later, Brenda came to Stockholm and stayed with me for a couple of weeks. We also befriended another young African-American, Bill Tatum. He was a writer who had been a Freedom Rider in the South, and was now living in Sweden. Bill later returned to America and became the editor of "New York Amsterdam News." I still keep in touch with him and his wife.

In some ways life was simple and easy in the early and mid-1960s. The world seemed more innocent then than now. Young people like us, not yet tied down by families, permanent jobs and other responsibilities were almost constantly on the road. Drugs were not yet available and I had never heard of hashish and marijuana. We lived cheaply, hitch-hiked everywhere and stayed in youth hostels. Thus we got to see large parts of the world, and created many friendships, some of them life-long.

After a few years I lost contact with Brenda. In 2001, through the miraculous Internet, I found her again. She was a professor of dance at a major university and had published several books. We were both delighted to talk on the phone after more than thirty years, and decided to meet soon in New York.

Shosh disappeared in the late 1960s. In 2003, after many years of searching, I found her, too, through the Internet. In the spring of 2004, she and her husband came all the way from London to see me in Florida where I now live. Shosh and I picked up our friendship where we had left it thirty-six years earlier, with no effort whatsoever. It was as though no time had passed. Our husbands also became good friends and we all had a wonderful time.

BERLIN

Peter had always been writing, as well as painting and making films. After years of writing in Swedish he had now reverted to German, his mother tongue. He was also spending more time in Germany, to reacquaint himself with the language, which had changed since he lived there in the 1930s.

In 1963 he started to write his first play, which was set around the time of the French Revolution. The inspiration came from a movie with Jean Paul Belmondo, about France in the 18th century, which we had all gone to see.

Peter worked on the play for over a year and gave it an excruciatingly long title: *The persecution and assassination of Jean Paul Marat as performed by the inmates of the Asylum of Charenton under the direction of the Marquis de Sade.* It was called *Marat/Sade* for short.

(Later the long name became subject to jokes like: "Have you seen Peter Weiss' play?" "No, but I read the title.")

In the spring of 1964, *Marat/Sade* had its world premiere at the Schiller Theatre in West Berlin. Gunilla, who was a versatile artist, had created the excellent stage design. Peter and Gunilla traveled to Berlin for the opening, and I was invited to come along.

It was very exciting for all of us. I got a new dress made of soft black silk especially for the opening night. Gunilla had picked it out for me, and she bought me a silk scarf in several shades of mauve and purple to go with the dress. For herself she had purchased a gorgeous grey-green velvet suit. A few hours before the opening we both went to the hairdresser and got elegant new hairstyles. Gunilla had always been good-looking, but in the velvet suit and her blonde hair piled high, she was stunning.

The play was a colossal success. At the end there was a fifteen-minute standing ovation, and Peter and Gunilla were called up on stage with the actors and director. The reviews the next day were splendid, calling the play sensational, a dramatic milestone of major importance. Peter, normally a sad person, was happy for once—he finally got the recognition he had longed for. I was enormously proud of him.

West Berlin was otherwise not a pleasant city. I perceived it as tasteless and gaudy. People with hard faces were talking loudly and affectedly in the cafés on Kurfürstendamm, the main boulevard. Huge signs advertised face-lifts and nose operations. There were pictures of long hooked noses that had become small and straight with plastic surgery. I got the feeling that large sums of money were squandered in this city and that unethical business transactions were occurring.

I visited a Jewish center and spoke to some young people there. I asked why their parents had voluntarily returned to Germany after the war. The young people had no sensible explanation for this, and said they were ashamed to live in Germany and would try to emigrate to Israel or America.

One day we went to East Berlin, as Peter was meeting friends there, and as you there could buy cheap books and records. It was my first visit to a city behind the iron curtain. East Berlin in its poverty was the opposite of West Berlin, but was awful and depressing in its own way. Instead of lavish ads for luxury items, the walls of buildings were covered with communist slogans, and there was an atmosphere of suspicion and apprehension. I felt sorry for the people who had to live in this grey, gloomy town.

Marat/Sade was translated into dozens of languages and performed all over the world. It received the Tony Award and many other awards. Even now, forty years later, *Marat/Sade* and other plays of Peter's are regularly performed, also in America. In England, *Marat/Sade* was made into a movie, directed by Peter Brook and starring Glenda Jackson.

Peter became more and more politically involved, and joined the Swedish Communist party. In 1967, together with Jean Paul Sartre, he took part in the Bertrand Russell Tribunal against the Vietnam War. He also visited Fidel Castro in Cuba.

He wrote many plays and novels, most of them with a strong political message. In the mid 1970s he published *The Aesthetics of Resistance*, a thousand-page novel in three parts that was hailed as another literary milestone. Now he was being considered for the Nobel Prize in Literature. In 1981 he was on the short list for the Prize, which finally went to Elias Canetti.

Although Peter was my father, or perhaps because he was my father, I had a hard time reading his books. The early autobiographical novels I could read, and I enjoyed *Marat/ Sade*. But the later works were beyond me—I just couldn't get through them. Some day I will try again.

OLOF

When I was twenty, I found another brilliant, blond, handsome and emotionally damaged young man, a student at the Stockholm University. His name was Olof Olofsson. We were too young to get married, but did so anyway. For both of us it was an attempt to find some stability and security in life.

Our wedding was celebrated at Rosenvik, the large and elegant home of Helga's mother Signe. There was a strange and strained mixture of guests at the party. Olof's parents were farmers from northern Sweden, good people, and very different from mine.

My family and friends were represented by about thirty people, most of them artists or scientists. Peter, who had written glowingly about the working class, was incapable of making conversation with the farmers. He didn't even try. Someone once remarked that Peter's only actual contact with the "lower classes" was with the taxi drivers, and this was probably true.

Helga, on the other hand, had always had a phenomenal ability to get along with all types of people, and became a good friend of Olof's family.

Olof's father and Helga's new husband, Ralf Parland,

withdrew to the cloak-room, where they emptied a bottle of whiskey. Olof's mother and siblings were huddling shyly in a corner. Channa (my friend from the kibbutz) and I danced the Hora, just the two of us. My grandmother Signe, who was then eighty years old, was sobbing with emotion over the newlyweds. She was also trying to be "folksy" and talk to the farmers "in their language" which was not very successful. She slapped Olof's father on the back and shouted "howdy"—a word she normally never used. The rest of my family was discussing politics and literature. Nobody thought our marriage would last, and they were right.

After the wedding, Olof and I flew to Las Palmas in the Canaries, a group of islands off the coast of North Africa. They were a popular tourist destination for northern Europeans, as the climate was warm and sunny even in winter.

It was our honeymoon, and one would think we would be happy in the Canaries. But Olof and I were both confused and unstable individuals. We often talked about the environment being unreal and "flat" like a picture, instead of three-dimensional—not only in Las Palmas, but anywhere. We were both getting therapy, but it didn't help. The tourist resort felt almost like a prison, and it was a relief to return to Stockholm after two weeks.

As predicted, our marriage lasted only a short time. I saw Olof again in the 1970s, but after that he vanished and severed all communication.

I was immature, careless and selfish when I was married to Olof, and sometimes I hurt him badly. I am truly sorry about this, and hope he will one day find it in his heart to forgive me.

FRANKFURT

By 1967 I was divorced from Olof. I had been three years at the art college, but then decided to go another route. Although I had always liked to paint I didn't feel I had anything important to communicate as an artist, and therefore I could just as well do something else. I now wanted to be a physician, and for that I needed to take some specific exams which would enable me to enter the university. Now I was back in a high school for adults, studying for my final exams.

In the 1960s in northern Europe practically every student, artist or intellectual was a socialist of some kind. We saw how masses of people were oppressed and exploited in large parts of the world—Asia, South America, Africa. We believed that socialism was the system that would rectify these injustices and ultimately create world peace. With the information and knowledge I had at the time, socialism seemed like a good thing.

The University of Frankfurt in Western Germany was considered the best place in Europe for social and political studies. The Professors Mitscherlich and Adorno, who taught there, were especially admired. I went to Frankfurt in the late spring of 1967 to spend the summer polishing up my German, and to attend some lectures at the university.

Through Peter's contacts I befriended a group of young German socialists. Peter was an idol of theirs, and therefore they immediately accepted me. It was a diverse group of students, all highly gifted and intelligent. Most of them were caring and sincere people, but some were high-strung and fanatic and reminded me of Nazis, although they were supposed to be just the opposite. There were also a few foreigners in the group, like Angela Davis, a black American girl. She was my age and had a huge "afro" hairstyle that I envied. Later she became a Black Panther, feminist and revolutionary.

There were continuous passionate discussions about politics and everything else. Since all the students were leftists, their opinions did not vary much. But when the Six Day War in Israel broke out in June, there was suddenly a difference of opinions. Some of the students liked Israel because of its kibbutzim and general socialism. They also felt guilty, as Germans, for what their parents had done to the Jews, and they therefore supported Israel. But many of them sided with the Palestinians, whom they considered oppressed, and they thought Israel should cease to exist.

For myself, my attention was only on the safety of my friends in Israel, especially the Levys and Fenigers, who had sons in the army. I prayed they would be all right.

One morning in the end of June, while sitting in class and waiting for Professor Mitscherlich to arrive, I fearfully opened a letter from my kibbutz. It had arrived just as I was leaving for the university. The letter, from Ruth Levy, stated that Ofer Feniger had been killed in the battle of Jerusalem.

The room started to spin. The floor was rocking. I almost fainted. Somehow I got out of the classroom and found my way back to my apartment. Frankfurt had suddenly lost its charm for me. University studies were no longer interesting. I was in a daze of grief and confusion, and returned to Sweden.

In Stockholm I embarked on a search for answers to the questions about life and death. It had become a vital necessity to understand what it was all about. Why was Ofer dead? What was the purpose of his short life? Why did I sometimes feel that he was standing right beside me? I could almost hear his voice! Was there a God, and if so, why did he permit so many tragedies to happen?

I had a burning need to talk about Ofer. I spoke to the Rabbi, who was a good man, but he had no consolation to give me. I spoke to a priest, who said it was "God's will" that Ofer had died, but that made no sense either. I wrote to people in Givat Chaim and everywhere else. I tried to discuss death with friends and family but nobody wanted to talk about it. The subject seemed to be taboo. I read books by Martin Buber and Erich Fromm, but still did not find what I was looking for.

Since neither the Jews nor the Christians nor the socialists had any answers, I started to look into other philosophies and religions, mainly Buddhism, Hinduism and Theosophy. Much of what I read made sense, like the concept of reincarnation.

SAINT HILL

Of the many people I wrote to, one sent a reply that caught my attention. This was an old friend who was now living in a place called Saint Hill in southern England. He said he had found some real answers to my questions about life and death. I was skeptical, but decided to check it out, and after finishing my pre-university exams in December 1967, I took the boat to England.

On New Year's Day of 1968 I arrived at Saint Hill. It was a college up in the hills outside a town named East Grinstead. Around the main buildings were attractive rose gardens and large green lawns. People there were studying Scientology, which meant "knowing how to know." It was a religious philosophy developed by the American L. Ron Hubbard. The atmosphere at Saint Hill was very good; everyone I met was cheerful and friendly.

The students at this college were learning to do a new kind of spiritual therapy, called "auditing," (from the Latin word "audire" which means "to listen"). They assured me it was not at all like dream analysis or free association. Auditing was based on a very different theory and was said to be extremely effective.

As part of their practical requirements, the students gave free auditing to anyone who wanted to try it. I had nothing to lose by giving it a go.

I sat down in a small room with one of the "auditors" in training. We were going to do a "session" which was the time period in which the auditing was delivered. The auditor asked me specific questions about a basic aspect of my life. The questions seemed simple, but interesting, and I answered as best I could. The auditor listened intently, never interrupted me, and seemed to truly understand what I was saying. He did not analyze my answers or voice his own opinions. These special questions encouraged me to really think, to look at things from many angles, and to find out what was true for me.

After a while I had a major realization about myself and my life, and felt a lot better. At that point the session was ended. It was not like psychoanalysis where the practitioner cuts you off after forty-five minutes, no matter how you are feeling.

For a couple of weeks I got one or two sessions a day. In each one I was asked new and different questions. The idea was always to strip away lies and confusions, to become more honest and aware. I began to see that every person is basically good and inherently knows what is true and right.

Ever since childhood I had been aware of a sort of grey fog around my head, like a wall between me and my surroundings. It had been numbing my emotions and preventing me from experiencing life fully. I thought this fog was "normal," an inevitable part of my existence.

After a week or so of auditing, this fog suddenly lifted. It was a physical experience—I could *feel* something lifting from my head—like having had a tight hat that was suddenly taken off.

It was the most spectacular thing that had ever happened

to me. When I looked around, all the colors were brighter. The environment was suddenly *real* and three-dimensional instead of flat like it normally was. The sad, depressed feeling that had always been with me was suddenly gone.

For the first time in my life, I was *happy*. It didn't hurt to live. Life no longer seemed dangerous and threatening. Instead of the usual self-hatred, I now started to like myself.

The closest I had been to happiness in the past had been when I was in love. Those moments of bliss had been brief and fragile and had always contained an element of fear. What I now experienced was a much higher level of happiness. It was a love of life and all people and a feeling of great freedom.

As the auditing continued, I got the answer to my questions about death. *There was no death.* I began to grasp that I was something more than just my body, and that I would continue to exist even if the body died. Had I not had a personal realization about this, I would never have believed it.

The concept of God also started to become real for me. I could see why this was a religion and not just a therapeutic method. Everything that was done had the purpose of increasing spiritual or religious awareness. It was called a church, because it was a congregation of people with a spiritual goal, but it was not a Christian church. People of all religions and races were welcomed and respected.

At Saint Hill there were dozens of other young people (and some older ones too) who had come to receive free auditing. They were searchers from all the European countries, from America, Australia, Africa and Israel, and most of them were walking on clouds just like I was.

Many visitors to Saint Hill, me included, did "the Communication Course" after the auditing. The first drill on this course was to simply sit on a chair opposite another student. We were instructed to sit and look at each other for two hours without talking or moving. At first it was difficult and uncomfortable to sit still like that. It was embarrassing, almost painful, to continuously look into the eyes of another person. But after some time I became calm and serene and able to be in the present. I felt it was the first time I had ever really looked at another human being. It was quite a revelation. The exercise was done with many different students, for several days. Eventually it didn't matter who was sitting in front of me, young or old, ugly or handsome. I began to see the beauty in each one of them.

My life had turned from night to day, and I was astonished. Naturally I became immensely interested in this new philosophy. What *was* it? How could these simple questions and simple drills have such a powerful effect on people?

I wanted to learn more about it, and to help others the way I had been helped. This was much more important than becoming a doctor. Therefore I went back to Sweden to save up money for a year of study at Saint Hill.

MORE TRIPS TO HELL

Back in Stockholm after a few weeks at Saint Hill, I told everybody about my wonderful experiences. I especially tried to describe them to Peter and Gunilla, who were such important persons in my life. I probably overwhelmed them and frightened them with my enormous enthusiasm, but I was young and immature and had not learnt how to best convey spiritual experiences to others.

Still, I had thought they would reason this way:

"Rebecca has had a rough childhood, very much because of *Peter*. Naturally she is searching for ways to heal herself. We should be grateful that she is not attempting suicide, is not criminal and is not on drugs like many of her friends and kids of her generation. If she wants to explore a new religion, let us give her a chance. Let us trust her and hope she made a good choice. If it is a bad choice she will soon find out by herself."

They did not reason that way. Peter and Gunilla said they had read several books about my new religion, and decided it was abhorrent. They viewed it in a very different way than I did. I felt they had completely misunderstood what the new philosophy was all about, and they felt I was brainwashed. All three of us were convinced we were right and the other party wrong.

Peter did everything in his power to get me out of Scientology. He raged and threatened, like Mutti used to do. He screamed that he would lock me up in a psychiatric hospital if he only could. That I was insane and would soon have a nervous breakdown. That he was ashamed of me and embarrassed to tell his friends what I was doing. When Helga tried to defend me, he yelled at her too until she burst out crying.

I was shocked and devastated by Peter's reaction. Over and over I tried to explain that the church had good intentions and had helped hundreds of thousands of people. But it was useless.

To be condemned by one's parents is just about the worst thing that can happen to a child, at least if one loves the parents. I had always loved Peter, in spite of his failures and irresponsibility, and I loved Gunilla. The greatest shock was that Gunilla, who had been closer to me than both Peter and Helga, suddenly did not understand me at all.

It wounded me deeply that they had no trust in me. They considered me incapable of making correct observations and sane decisions, even later when decades had passed and anyone could see that I was doing well in life. I had not become psychotic; neither was I fanatic or dogmatic.

For a while I tried to solve the problem by disconnecting from them. This was a big mistake, for which I later profusely apologized, but it was very upsetting for Peter when it happened.

Sometimes I refused to discuss the new religion with them, sometimes I wrote them angry letters accusing them of trying to ruin my life. This was stupid of me and just made matters worse. I don't think they ever forgave me for these mistakes. Later I realized that they, like most parents, probably did what they thought was best. They wanted to protect me from something they honestly believed was dangerous. But in those years I couldn't understand their viewpoint, any more than they could understand mine.

Every visit to their house was like a trip to hell. I felt like a pariah in my own family and always left their home depressed. Our good relationship was destroyed. The only way for me to repair it would have been to leave the new religion. But I had to do what was right for me—I could not change my life and convictions just to please them.

Helga, on the other hand, had quite a different reaction. Instead of listening to other people's opinions, she decided to personally experience Scientology and make up her own mind. She went to Saint Hill, got some auditing herself, with good results, and had long talks with the staff members. Helga did not join the church, but always accepted it and supported me. I admired her tolerance and integrity.

When Peter was young he had also made a choice that his parents strongly opposed. He wanted to be an artist, but Daddy tried to force him in a different direction, and Mutti tore up one of his paintings. Now he was just as harsh to his own child.

The breach with Peter and Gunilla is the greatest tragedy of my life. During the 1970s we met only a few times. On Christmas Eve 1978 I was in their apartment. A photo of Peter and his three biological children was then taken—it is the only existing picture of the four of us together.

Although Peter in 1981 responded in a reasonably friendly way to one of my letters, and although Gunilla and I were on civilized terms the few times we met, the relationship was never the same again. Not until 2002, in connection with Helga's death, did my relationship with Gunilla slowly start to normalize. I hope and pray that it will one day be fully restored.

I have thought a lot about this over the years. Why this kind of catastrophe has to happen, not just in my life but in many others. I am thinking of the Jewish family that shatters when the son marries a shiksa (a gentile girl). The daughter who becomes a communist and denounces her conservative parents. The mother who condemns her son because he joined Hare Krishna.

All these family members could have enriched each other's lives with many years of good communication, respect and understanding. Instead they often go to their graves without reconciliation. Why do we have so little tolerance for each other?

APOLLO

In spite of the opposition from Peter and Gunilla, I studied a year at Saint Hill. I was on course eight hours a day, six days a week, learning to apply to others the kind of therapy I had received myself. The courses were engrossing. When the training was completed I worked a few years as an auditor in California and Sweden. It gave me great satisfaction to help others improve their lives.

In 1971 I spent several months aboard the Apollo, the ship where L Ron Hubbard was the Commodore. There he lived and worked together with a group of dedicated assistants. During this time I saw Ron many times, at staff meetings and in private encounters. Sometimes he exchanged a few words with me, asking how I was doing. *Really* asking, not just out of politeness. This was his most striking quality—the ability to really be there and really talk to people. I have never, before or after, met anyone who had such an ability to communicate. He was a remarkable man and I am glad I had the opportunity to meet him.

Peter Weiss, Helga Henschen and Randi Rebecca by
Peter's painting *Life around an old Palazzo*, 1944

Peter in the Stockholm archipelago, 1944

Rebecca, 1949

Helga, 1946

Party at the Robber's
drawing by Helga Henschen

Daddy (Eugen Weiss)

Folke Henschen
Helga's father

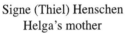

Signe (Thiel) Henschen
Helga's mother

Mutti (Franziska Weiss) as a
young woman in a role portrait

The house of Mutti and Daddy in Alingsås

Mutti and Rebecca, 1945

Daddy and Rebecca, 1946

Self-portrait made by Peter for Rebecca's poetry album, 1952

Watercolor by Ingrid Vang Nyman for Rebecca's poetry album, 1956

Peter and Rebecca, 1952

Helga by one of her sculptures in the 1950s

Rebecca in Alhambra, 1955
(photo: Emilio Ruiz)

Gunilla Palmstierna, 1953
(photo: Wilma Björling)

A.S. Neill and Ena Neill, Summerhill 1960

Channa Bankier, 1965

Ofer Feniger, ca. 1966

Tana Ross with daughter Joana, late 1960s

Amnon Levy
ca. 1961

Brenda Dixon, Greer Johnson, Rebecca, 1963

Olof and Rebecca, 1965 (photo: Willier)

Wedding photo. Back row: Olof's mother, Olof, Rebecca, Olof's father. Front row: Ralf Parland, Helga, Gunilla, Peter

Sri Lanka, oil painting by Rebecca

Love, lithograph by Rebecca

Rebecca, 1980
(photo: R. Mansfield)

Rebecca in Leningrad, USSR, 1984

Peter, Nadja, Paul, Rebecca Weiss, 1978
(photo: Gunilla)

Creating a Universe
appliqué by Rebecca

Solomon's Garden
appliqué by Rebecca

Mediterranean Village
appliqué by Rebecca

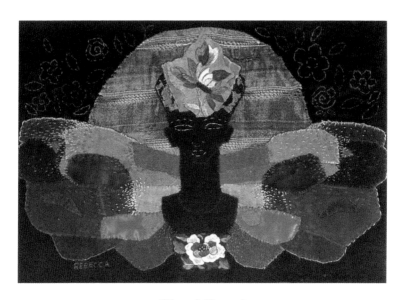

Winged Pharaoh
appliqué by Rebecca

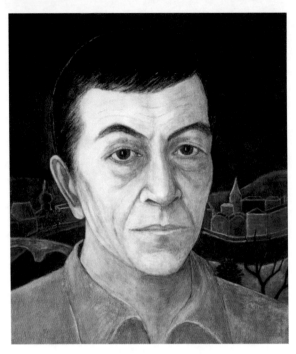

Portrait of Peter, painting by Rebecca, 1982

Portrait of Suzanne Osten, painting by Rebecca, 1980s

Wim, Vic, Stu, Rebecca, Marije Sjouwerman in France, 1993

Helga in Stockholm, 1996 (photo: Anders Fugelstad)

Nadja, 1997

Stu and Rebecca, 2000
(photo: Sam Licciardi)

Miguel and Natasha in Big Bend National Park, 2001

Miguel and Natasha in their camper, 2001

Carmelito in Terlingua

The Weisz family, ca. 1900:
Eugen (Daddy), his mother Fanny, sister Aranka,
brother Edmund, sister Malvine, father Moritz

Lisa (Weisz) Gewing
Peter's cousin, 2001

Helga, February 2002
(photo: Elisabeth Auer)

Animals Resting,
oil painting by Helga, 1980s

Watercolor by Helga, June 2002

ERIK

I met Erik in the early 1970s. Erik was a blond Swede with an IQ of 150. He was a complicated man, but uncommonly able and dynamic, and highly spiritually aware.

Erik was the first person who had ever really *seen* me and come to know me in a profound way. (Ron had seen me too, but in a more general way, like he saw everyone he spoke to.) Erik had a unique ability to zero in on me as a spiritual being. He could see beyond my problems and confusions and see the essence in me that was infinite, that transcended my body and present life. When Erik saw me and recognized me, I understood who I really was. It was as earth-shaking as my time at Saint Hill. No words can describe the exhilaration of truly being seen by another person. There is nothing else like it. If it were the only good thing that had ever happened to me, this experience alone would have made my life worthwhile.

Very few have the ability or willingness to see others. Most people are so entangled in their own problems that they don't have the time or strength to see and listen to others. You need to have a stillness in yourself to be able to concentrate on another person, and so few of us have such inner stillness. Erik had it at times, and then we would talk all through the night. The communication was life-changing for me and so fantastic for both of us that we forgot to eat and sleep. We also wrote long, poetic letters to each other although we met every day.

In the physical world we made a trip to Sri Lanka, a large island southeast of India. In 1974 it was still called Ceylon. We were both interested in Hinduism and Buddhism, and Sri Lanka was a good place to study these cultures and religions.

The flight from Stockholm took almost twenty-four hours, including stopovers in Turkey and Pakistan. Paradoxically, I had begun to develop a fear of flying, even though I knew it was illogical. It wasn't death itself I was afraid of, it was the fire and agony of an air crash. The minute we landed I calmed down.

Sri Lanka was a very crowded island. Not even half the size of Florida, or a quarter of Sweden, it had fourteen million inhabitants. They were friendly and eager to talk to foreigners and tourists. Since they spoke English, language was not a problem.

It was interesting to see a culture so different from the European. Religion was part of the daily lives and general awareness of the people. They believed implicitly in reincarnation and talked about it casually, as a natural fact of life. Although they were poor and lived simple lives they seemed happier and more peaceful than people in the West.

The island had majestic mountains, large tea plantations, and endless beaches. In the city of Anuradapura, which dated back to 400 BC, there was a holy tree. It had grown from a shoot of the tree Buddha sat under when he had his religious visions. A temple had been built around it, and Buddhists from many countries made pilgrimages to this place. Near the city were giant statues of Buddha, carved out of the rocks.

Not far from Anuradapura was Sigiriya, a peculiar, very

steep mountain, which we climbed. Near the top were grottos with exquisite mural paintings made in the sixth century.

There was lush vegetation everywhere on the island—white orchids, pink rhododendrons, mango trees, ferns and palms. Elephants walked in the streets and hundreds of monkeys climbed in the trees. The women wore silk saris in luminous colors, and the monks were glowing in their orange robes. It was a joy to look at, and inspired many later paintings.

Shortly after we came back to Sweden, Erik stepped out of my life. He married another girl and moved to Denmark. From time to time I heard about him through mutual friends. In the 1980s I met him once and we and talked for a few hours, but after that I never saw him again.

In January 2002 Erik died of cancer, only fifty-five years old. I had no idea he had been ill, and was shocked when I heard the news.

Somehow I had always hoped to eventually rekindle my friendship with Erik. I had once lived with him and almost married him, but it wasn't that part of the relationship I missed. It was the communication with Erik as a human and spiritual being.

I wished he had sent me a farewell letter. Another friend, when she was dying a few years earlier, wrote to me about her illness. She thanked me for our friendship, and said she hoped to see me in another life. It was a comfort to get such a letter, and made it easier to accept the message of her death when it later arrived.

In any case I sent my condolences to Cecilia, Erik's widow. I did not expect her to answer, as we had not liked each other in the 1970s. At that time I resented her for "stealing" Erik from me, but in the vicinity of death such pettiness evaporates. To my surprise Cecilia replied, and we started a friendly correspondence.

In the autumn of 2002 I visited Cecilia in Sweden, where she now lived. I met her and Erik's daughters who were in their twenties and sharp and witty just like Erik. Cecilia emanated a warmth and kindness that I had never anticipated, and we became very good friends. Getting to know these three women was wonderful. Not a trace of our hostility from the 1970s remained. We all felt that Erik was present in our meeting and that he was happy for us.

ARTISTIC AND SPIRITUAL JOURNEYS

My experiences at Saint Hill and with Erik had given me a tremendous artistic boost. I now had something important to say about the spiritual side of life, and started to paint again.

I had come to understand that artists can greatly influence society, and therefore have a huge responsibility. Artists have to open doors, show roads out of the human misery. Our culture and civilization can be raised and improved if we keep giving hope, keep showing the beauty and decency of man. If we remind people of their true nature, they will become more ethical and live better lives. It was my responsibility to contribute to the positive forces in the world.

There were also other sources of inspiration, like music by Mozart and Beethoven, and certain books I read and re-read. *Winged Pharaoh,* a poetic novel by Joan Grant, inspired many paintings and appliqués. Grant wrote about a female Pharaoh who lived in Egypt four thousand years ago and who had supernatural powers.

The journeys in outer space of Saint-Exupery's *Little Prince* were still as marvelous as they had been in my childhood. When I read the Song of Songs in the Bible I got a stream of visions and ideas, especially after having lived in Israel and seen the vineyards, pomegranates and blooming almond trees.

Even Helga was a source of inspiration. By this time we had completely repaired our relationship. Through auditing I had learned not to blame others for what happened in my life, and Helga had become increasingly wise and understanding. Although I was no longer bitter about my childhood, Helga kept making amends in various ways. I was amazed that she realized her mistakes, and tried to repair the damage. Many fathers and mothers of my friends had been even worse as parents than mine, but had no thought of amends. Instead they justified the harmful acts they had done, and got angry when their children criticized them.

Helga however was developing a personal greatness. She was willing to take responsibility for all that had happened and did everything in her power to help and support me. She had also become actively involved in several humanitarian and charitable organizations, helping both people and animals.

As an artist she was flourishing. Her paintings and poems were often of world class, and they inspired me in my own work. In 1975 Helga completed her largest commission, an underground station in Stockholm. She spent two years filling the station with her sculptures, paintings and poetry. I admired Helga as an artist and human being and felt blessed to have such a mother. Helga said *I* was also an inspiration for *her*, and dedicated several books to me.

EAST GRINSTEAD

In 1979 I got married again, to Tomas Berger, whom I had met in Stockholm. He was born in Germany, but had immigrated to Sweden a few years earlier. Tomas had a terrific sense of humor, and from him I learned how to laugh and see the comical side of life.

Tomas received a job offer in East Grinstead, England, and we decided to go and live there for a while. I hadn't been there for ten years and was glad to return.

The countryside in southern England has a special charm. It has rolling hills, is lush and green and dotted with small towns and villages, most of them several hundred years old. They have cobblestone streets, ancient churches and an abundance of quaint and picturesque pubs.

East Grinstead is one of these small southern towns. Its center was built in the 14th century, and in 1979 it had about twenty thousand inhabitants. It was an hour by train from London, and an hour and a half from Brighton on the south coast. The trains to London ran several times a day. Surrounding East Grinstead were meadows, fields and forests. One was the Ashdown Forest, where the writer A.A. Milne used to live, and which is the setting for his books about Winnie the Pooh. Saint Hill was nearby, and in Forest Row, a neighboring village, was a Steiner college for adult Anthroposophy students.

Tomas' job was poorly paid and we had very little money. We drove an old Volkswagen that kept breaking down. It had to be parked on a hill at night so that it could be rolled down in the morning—that was the only way it would start. We lived frugally in an old house that we shared with friends, and we had two cats that I cherished. (Our friends adopted the cats when we later left England.) I had a small studio where I made my appliqués and paintings.

Good and bad things happened during those years. The worst was that I had an ectopic pregnancy, lost the baby and almost lost my life. I really wanted a child and had tried a long time to get pregnant. When I finally succeeded, it ended in this painful way. I never managed to get pregnant again, and the stress and sorrow connected with this is one of the reasons our marriage did not last. But Tomas and I remained friends after the divorce in 1983, and we still are.

We considered adoption, but somehow it did not happen. Eventually I resigned myself to the fact that I would not be a mother, and would have to direct my creativity into other areas of life. What helped me get over the grief was my conviction that I had lived before and would live again. I think I have had children in the past and perhaps will have them in the future.

The best thing that happened was that I helped create a group of artists. It was a joy and surprise to discover that there were several superb young artists living in East Grinstead. Freddy Hall, an Englishman who was already quite well known, made rare and delicate sculptures and jewelry. His wife Sherry was a multi-talented artist, as was Horst Kramer, a German painter with an American wife. Then there was Ellen de Groot, a Dutch girl who made magnificent water colors. Her enigmatic images were like nothing I had ever seen. I am proud to still own a couple of her paintings as well as a tiny sculpture of Freddy's.

Gradually I got to know these artists, and we started to meet a couple of times a week to talk about art. We showed our work to each other and got feedback and constructive criticism. Horst taught me new oil painting techniques. His wife Melanie and I planned mutual activities, exhibitions and marketing. We called ourselves the Grinstead Group.

I found that my purpose with art was not only for myself, but to help other artists and groups who create beautiful things and positively influence society.

How can I explain the thrill of communicating and working with other artists? There is a mutual reality that is vital and precious. It is a marvel to see their works unfolding and to experience the universes and viewpoints that are uniquely theirs and are so skillfully and sensitively expressed. Few things in life are more exciting than looking at a true and original piece of art. It creates an impact in your soul and heart. It opens new vistas and inspires you endlessly.

Our program stated: "The Grinstead Group consists of five artists from four countries who met in the English town of East Grinstead in 1979 and formed a group for the purposes of mutual help, exchange of ideas and combined projects. They convey an essentially spiritual message, one which transcends individual cultural backgrounds and seeks a higher level of connection between artist and viewer."

I presented our group to museums and galleries in Sweden. As a result we had a 1982 exhibition at "Glas," one of the best galleries in Stockholm. It was very successful and we appeared in a cultural program on national TV. The next year Melanie organized a show for us in Los Angeles, and twice I showed with Ellen in another Stockholm gallery.

Sadly enough I lost contact with the Grinstead Group members. The group dissolved when I moved back to Sweden and Ellen to Holland. It is my dream to one day have a new group of artists.

PETER

While living in England, I had some correspondence with Peter. I was still desperately trying to improve our relationship, and he finally seemed to have mellowed somewhat. In June of 1981 he was still very critical of me, but wrote: "I am aware that I failed you when you were a child and needed me." That was the closest he had ever come to an apology.

Tomas and I returned to Stockholm in April 1982 and I was actually looking forward to seeing Peter again. I was planning to visit him, but waited too long. On May 10th I was awakened by a phone call in the middle of the night. Peter had died of a sudden heart attack. He was only sixty-five years old.

Gunilla discouraged me from seeing Peter's body, but I went to the hospital anyway. Without seeing the body I would never believe he was dead and would not be able to say good-bye to him.

When I arrived at 4:00 a.m. he was already in the morgue, and I went down there. I was shaking, still in a state of shock. At my request they moved Peter to a small chapel where I could be alone with him. I sat by his body and cried for a long time. His pale face will be forever imprinted in my memory.

Many people came to Peter's funeral. Some came from other countries, like his Suhrkamp publisher and some foreign journalists. The ceremony was in a non-denominational church, without any religious elements. Among the speakers were C.H. Hermansson, the leader of the Swedish Communist party, and the actor Stellan Skarsgård, who read a piece from *The Aesthetics of Resistance.*

Nadja, my half-sister who was only nine years old, sat silently in her white dress by Gunilla's side. I was sorry she had lost her father at such a young age. Micke, my stepbrother, sat quiet and withdrawn on her other side. My half-brother Paul, who had come up from Denmark where he lived, sat next to Helga and me. His own mother could not attend.

Arwed (Peter's half-brother on Mutti's side) and his daughter Carola arrived from Berlin, and my cousins Stig and Karin from Alingås. Their mother Irene was too ill to travel.

After the funeral there were two gatherings. One was for Peter's and Gunilla's closest friends, at a neighbor's house. The other was for Peter's siblings and their families, in Helga's home. Even Peter's brother, Alexander, who had just suffered a stroke, came there in his wheelchair with his daughter Katri.

The best part of that gathering, for me, was to rekindle my friendship with Stig and Karin, warm and loving people whom I had not seen since childhood. All of us talked about Peter and shared our memories.

I had mixed feelings about Peter's death. I couldn't help grieving, and was very sad that we had not been fully reconciled before he died. I felt that he had failed me again by dying too early—that he had sort of sneaked away. But it was also a relief that he was gone. In some way, a heavy burden and huge problem had lifted from my shoulders.

LENINGRAD

In 1984 the Soviet Union still existed. The Iron Curtain was thoroughly drawn and there was very little communication between the USSR and the western world. It was known, however, that many Soviet citizens, especially the Jews, were oppressed and abused.

One September day in 1984, when I was living in Stockholm, I was approached in a very secretive way by an Israeli agent. He must have been a member of the Mossad, the Israeli Secret Service, although he did not say so. A friend of mine had given him my phone number. I was called to a meeting with both of them in an obscure apartment in a suburb.

The agent, who called himself Moshe, swore me to secrecy regarding this meeting. Then he gave me a briefing on the condition of the Jews in the USSR. He told me that most of them were forbidden to emigrate to Israel. If they applied for a visa to leave the country, they lost their jobs and were denied new employment. They were not allowed to practice their religion, celebrate their culture or learn Hebrew. Some were deported to Siberia where they often froze or starved to death. They lived in poverty and misery, isolated from the rest of the planet. The Soviet newspapers were heavily censored and printed mostly lies and propaganda, and the Jews were yearning for real news and contact with the world.

Moshe said the Soviet Jews needed information about Israel and international events that concerned them. A secret information line had been set up, going from Europe to the USSR, via Scandinavia. Messengers were frequently traveling between Stockholm and Leningrad (now called St. Petersburg), pretending to be tourists. They smuggled in news and Hebrew literature to the Soviet Jews. New messengers were constantly needed, as it would create suspicion if the same faces were seen over and over.

He asked me if I was willing to make such a trip. My expenses would be paid. When I inquired about the danger involved, Moshe admitted there was a small risk of getting caught and sent to a Soviet prison. He urged me to go anyway, appealing to my solidarity and compassion with these oppressed people. But I am a pretty cowardly person, and the idea of being imprisoned in the USSR, and maybe sent to Siberia, was terrifying. I didn't have the nerve to do it, so I declined, feeling very guilty.

Tomas and I were now divorced, but still close friends. I broke my promise to the agent and told Tomas about the proposal. Tomas liked the idea and thought it would be a great adventure! He is not even Jewish but admired the brave dissidents in Russia and was willing to make this trip with me.

Going with Tomas made the trip "confrontable" for me, and we decided to take the plunge. I managed to contact Moshe, the agent, and a meeting was set up for the three of us. Moshe gave us a small microfilm with Hebrew text, supposedly containing information about an international Jewish convention that had recently taken place. The film was sewn into the hem of Tomas' trousers.

We were thoroughly drilled on where to go and what to do in Leningrad. Everything had to be memorized as we couldn't carry any maps, names or addresses. We were also given a cover story to tell the authorities in case we were caught.

In October Tomas and I joined a weekend charter trip to Leningrad. It was on a cruise ship, and organized by the Soviet Tourist Bureau. We had received a temporary visa to enter the USSR. The trip from Stockholm took about twenty-four hours.

Arriving at the Leningrad customs and passport control, we perceived a tense and threatening atmosphere. The customs officials wore military uniforms and grim facial expressions. There were mirrors in the ceiling and on the sides of each customs booth. Every woman's handbag was opened and examined. Every man's jacket and pockets were checked. While they were searching Tomas I nearly fainted with fear. I already had visions of Tomas and me arrested by the KGB, interrogated, tortured and sent to Siberia. But they did not find the microfilm, and I was immensely relieved.

Our group of tourists was housed in what was considered the best hotel in town, but it was no more than a two-star, by European standards. The food in the hotel restaurant was barely edible. Our Russian guide, who had learned Swedish at the Leningrad University, was present at all times and watched us like a hawk. No one was allowed to leave the group and the pre-arranged excursions.

Tomas and I had to somehow get away from the group. After dinner on the first evening the group was supposed to go to a circus. On our way there I pleaded a migraine and the guide reluctantly allowed Tomas and me to return to the hotel by ourselves. When the guide was out of sight we sneaked into a nearby underground station, where we got on a train, which we hoped was the right one. The other passengers studied us in hostile and covert ways. They could see we were foreigners although we tried to blend in by wearing simple and inexpensive clothes.

We had memorized which station to go to, but the names of the stations were written in Russian, which has a different alphabet than ours. We had to practically guess at where to exit.

Somehow we found the right suburb, and found our way in the dark to a dilapidated ten-story building. It was very slum-like and had no lights or functioning elevators. We climbed to the fifth floor and knocked on an unmarked door—the second door to the left, as Moshe had told us. The door was immediately opened and a woman rushed us inside without a word.

In this tiny, rundown apartment without a shower or bathtub, lived a large Jewish family. The husband, Yaakov, had been a successful engineer, but had lost his job when he applied for an emigration visa to Israel. The visa was denied and he was therefore a "refusenik." He now had to make a living with odd jobs like cleaning toilets in parks and hospitals. With his meager income he had to support his wife, three children and parents-in-law, who were all living with him. Yaakov was also a Hebrew teacher and was secretly giving lessons. He spoke a little English, and since I still spoke decent Hebrew, we were able to communicate.

The whole family was overjoyed to see us. In spite of their flagrant poverty they offered us tea and cookies. The microfilm was removed from Tomas' pants, and Yaakov gave us another film to take back to Europe. He didn't say how he had received that film or what it contained. We talked about an hour about their situation and about world news. Yaakov wanted us to meet another Jewish man the next day, a well-known dissident. He told us to be by the Pushkin statue at 1:00 p.m. We parted with the ancient Jewish saying: "Leshana habaah be Yerushalayim" (Until next year in Jerusalem). The whole visit was extremely moving and we were all close to tears when we said good-bye.

Next day we managed to sneak away for a few minutes after lunch, and went to the nearby Pushkin statue. The dissident was not there. Instead Yaakov showed up and whispered to us that he man we were going to meet had been arrested early that morning and sent to Siberia. Then Yaakov disappeared.

Tomas and I spent one more day in Leningrad, sightseeing. The main square with gigantic pictures of Marx, Engels and Lenin was overwhelming. Hundreds of soldiers with solemn faces were marching there, back and forth. In the Hermitage Art Museum, which had once been the palace of the Tsar, we saw marvelous paintings by my favorite artists, Gauguin and Rousseau. But the whole city was grey, both physically and spiritually. People in the street were unsmiling. The political oppression was tangible. There were no restaurants or movie theatres, even in the very centre of town, and the few shops we saw were small and practically empty of merchandise. One grocery store was open. It carried only white cabbage, potatoes and canned soup.

When we left the Soviet Union we were again searched by the customs people and again they did not find the film. I was greatly relieved when our ship steered out of the harbor.

Back in Sweden we delivered Yaakov's film to the agent. We were thoroughly debriefed, and thanked on behalf of the State of Israel.

It struck me again that Israel does a remarkable job of helping endangered Jews all over the world. Its operations in the former USSR, in Yemen, in Entebbe and other places are mind-boggling. What other country helps its Diaspora in a similar way?

Later I read in the paper about members of Jehovah's Witnesses who had smuggled bibles to the USSR. They had been caught and imprisoned for years. Tomas and I had been lucky.

Around 1989 I heard that Yaakov and his family had finally been allowed to leave Russia, and that made me very,

very happy. Maybe not next year, but some day, I will run into them in Jerusalem.

In 1992 I got another opportunity to support the Russian Jews, when the Jewish Center in Stockholm commissioned me to make a lithograph for them. The edition, of 150 signed copies, was sold through the Center. The whole profit went to "Exodus 92," to help Russian Jews immigrate to Israel.

STU

The next few years were spent mostly in Stockholm. I painted many portraits and got several large commissions. One was a triptych appliqué for Sundbyberg City Hall, another was a 7- by 20-foot wall hanging for Serafen Hospital in Stockholm. Yet another was a large mural painting for Scandinavian Airline Systems, in their new headquarters at the Stockholm airport.

In 1988 I spent six months on the west coast of Florida. There I met Stu Sjouwerman, a tall, blue-eyed Dutchman with a kind and sunny disposition. Since I had grown up among many neurotic and sarcastic people, it was a joy to be with Stu, who was so different. I fell deeply in love with him and told Helga on the phone that I had finally met a man who was not neurotic. Helga did not believe such men existed and every time I called her she asked: "Hasn't he had a fit of rage yet?" (All men Helga knew sooner or later had fits of rage.) This became a standing joke, and Stu, who has clown talents, would sometimes pretend he had a fit when Helga called. He would growl and scream in the background so that Helga would hear it, and later when she visited us he threw himself on the floor and hammered with his fists on the carpet in a simulated fit. Helga would then always go into stitches.

Stu allowed me to be exactly as I was and never criticized me. If I said or did something stupid he paid no attention to it and did not comment. His philosophy was that things which are bad or wrong tend to dissolve by themselves if you don't react back or make a big deal out of them. It was exceedingly therapeutic to be treated this way. Criticism and revenge just make things worse. If instead you admire and encourage all the good things about each other, both people will flourish. Everybody should apply these simple rules on their family and friends.

After knowing each other a few months, we got married. I swore to myself that this time, the marriage was going to last. We were hoping to settle in America, but it was impossible to get work permits, so we returned to Europe.

PARIS

We were excited when in 1989 Stu was offered a job in Paris. He would get an executive post in an international software company and we would live in The Most Beautiful City In The World.

The company, Sunbelt Software, was situated in a suburb, Rueil Malmaison. We rented an apartment a few minutes' walk from the office. There was no point in getting a car, because it is suicide to drive in Paris and in many of its suburbs, and there are no parking spaces.

I also got a job at Sunbelt, part-time. I chose this in order to experience and better understand Stu's world. He had been working with computers since the 1970s, but I knew nothing about them.

After my two earlier failed marriages, I had finally found the right kind of man for me. Or maybe I should say: I had finally become the kind of woman a sane man could stand to live with. In auditing I had worked on my self-destructive tendencies, and had actually reached a point where I knew I was able to create a good marriage without compulsively trying to destroy it.

By whatever good luck or good sense I had found Stu. He

is a treasure of a person—bright, loving, faithful and ethical. I knew that men like Stu don't grow on trees, and I wanted to do everything in my power to make the marriage work.

I spent the mornings at Sunbelt. In the afternoons I sat in our small apartment making paintings and appliqués, which I regularly brought back to Sweden to exhibit and sell.

Stu blossomed in his job, but I felt stifled at Sunbelt. The boring office work and interacting with people I had nothing in common with was depressing. Nobody in the office or among Stu's colleagues shared my interests or view on life and I felt dreadfully out of place. The only fun part was when I helped organize international conventions. There was a successful one in Cannes in southern France, attended by delegates from many countries. We all stayed in the famous Carlton Hotel and ate in the best restaurants. Coming from a socialist family I felt somewhat uncomfortable and embarrassed in these places, but couldn't help enjoying the luxury.

Stu loved Paris. I loved Stu and we had an excellent relationship but I was not happy. I tried to make friends among the Parisians, but my French was bad the first couple of years, and most Parisians spoke poor English. They were disinterested, not to say hostile, to foreigners. I was hardly ever invited to anybody's home, and found very few French people who were on my wavelength or willing to get to know me. This was shocking, because I had never before had trouble making new friends. Eventually I established friendships with two able, creative women, Marie Dominique and Noelle, but they were exceptions.

During the last of our four years in Paris, when I was no longer employed in Sunbelt, life became more enjoyable. I bought weekly passes on the metro, buses and local trains, and began touring Paris and its suburbs by myself, while Stu was working.

It was a pleasure to see the exquisite architecture, fascinating historical sites and many enchanting districts of Paris. I toured the river Seine that meandered through the city; the Left Bank and Boulevard St Michel with its art galleries, open-air cafés and second hand book stores; the steep hills of Sacre Coeur and Montmartre; the bustling streets and markets by the Bastille; the Louvre and the Museum of the Impressionists. The surroundings of Paris were as breathtaking as the city. Suburbs like the ancient St-Germain-en-Laye or the brand new La Defense are astounding. I always felt elated during these solitary tours. I could write a book about all these places, but so many others have written about Paris.

Some weekends we rented a car and drove to other parts of France. One time we went down to the Loire valley, where most of the medieval castles are. The Chambord castle from the 1500s is like something from another planet. I had never seen such resplendent and almost surreal architecture. We also noticed that the French people in the countryside and smaller towns were much friendlier than the Parisians.

In spite of my partly negative experiences in Paris, I did accomplish what I had aimed for. I did get acquainted with Stu's world of business and software, and this has probably contributed to the stable and happy marriage we still have.

One single truly important bond was made in Paris. This was with Jo Murciano, the owner of Sunbelt. A skilled and ethical businessman, with a charming wife, he became Stu's friend, mentor and partner.

In 1993, with Jo's help, Stu was able to start a branch of Sunbelt in America. This made it possible for us to move back to Florida. Our lives have been linked to Jo's for many years now, and he frequently visits us and the Florida office. We are always delighted to see him.

AMSTERDAM

Stu was born and raised in Amsterdam, and we have been to Holland many times. While I don't speak Dutch, I can easily communicate with the inhabitants, as most of them speak English, German or French. Stu speaks all four languages.

The Sjouwermans live near Amsterdam. Stu's parents Vic (Victoria) and Wim (Willem) have been happily married since the 1950s. They are always kind and considerate with each other and with their friends and family. Stu's two sisters and his brother also have good marriages and are doing well in life. The parents, children and grandchildren are very close and like to spend time together. There are never any major or lasting conflicts.

When I see Vic and Wim, I understand why Stu is the way he is. He had a stable, harmonious childhood. His parents love him and trust him and have given him a lot of freedom. They let him live his own life but are always there for him.

Holland on the whole is probably the most tolerant country in the world, for better or worse.

Prostitution has been legal in Holland since 1911. One

time, when Stu and I were in Amsterdam in the 1990s, we visited the Red Light district. Prostitutes were sitting in windows, displaying themselves as pieces of merchandise. They were half naked, and were sewing or reading while waiting for customers. When a customer came, they drew the curtains and turned on a red light, to show that they were busy. Mixed into the Red Light district were the special "Coffee Shops," where you could legally buy small portions of hashish and marijuana.

Euthanasia for terminally ill people is legal, as are same-sex marriages.

Holland has always been tolerant to its minorities. The country opened up to Jews in the 1400s and has treated them well ever since. During World War II, when the Germans invaded Holland and deported many Jews to concentration camps, something very unusual happened. The Dutch dock workers took to the streets and actually demonstrated en masse, shouting: "We want our bloody Jews back!" Dutch people hid and helped many Jews, such as Anne Frank, during the war.

I like the medieval districts in Amsterdam, the winding canals, and the Rembrandt and Van Gogh museums. But most of all I like Amsterdam because it is Stu's city.

FLORIDA

It was a relief to move to America after four years in Paris. Life in Florida is easy and relaxed. The climate is pleasant and the cost of living low.

I miss seeing forests and mountains, but there are long white beaches in Florida, and flowers blooming in winter.

People here are friendly, open and easygoing. Gradually we established a circle of close friends—artists, writers, medical and business people. Many of them are involved in alternative health and environmental issues.

Stu worked with skill and persistence to create Sunbelt USA. It did well and grew steadily. After a couple of years we had green cards, and in 2002 we built our own house in the town of Belleair in Pinellas County. We have a large garden with pines, oaks, orange, grapefruit and banana trees, and I keep planting new seedlings. The trees have become my friends, and in the springtime I check on them daily. I talk to them, encourage and admire them.

I started to teach once a week at a local art centre. It has three or four galleries, a museum, a gift shop, and studios where all the arts and crafts are taught. I participate in shows at the centre, and in other galleries and museums.

Stu helped me set up an Internet web site. There I show the

works of several painters, not just my own. This is the closest I have come to forming a new group of artists, my dream ever since I lost the Grinstead Group.

I did find an Israeli folk dance group. The teacher Jeana is gentle and patient and dedicated to her art. The students are both Jews and Gentiles and of all ages. Some of the dances are new, invented by modern Israeli choreographers. Some are old and classic like Maim and Tzena, and some are Hassidic. They are all light and graceful, and the music exhilarating.

There are many problems and conditions to criticize in America, but it is still the best country I have lived in. It has the best constitution. There is more freedom here, and more possibilities for the individual than anywhere else in the world. There is tolerance for minorities and religions, and Jews are not persecuted. I like America and am grateful to be here.

STOCKHOLM

I am terrified of airplanes and had managed to avoid them for years. I only fly when it is a matter of life and death. In May 1997 Helga had become very ill, and the dreaded moment came—I had to fly to Sweden. I was Helga's only child, and cared about her greatly. A trip by boat and train would have taken more than a week, and was therefore out of the question.

Statistics on air travel safety mean nothing to me. As far as I am concerned, there is a 50% chance that my plane will crash. So I put my affairs in order, wrote my will, and made a list of other important information Stu would need if I were no longer around.

Stu (who flies all the time and loves it) drove me to Tampa airport and I took my last farewell of him. I got on the plane and downed a small whiskey bottle that I had bought at the airport. Since I normally don't drink alcohol I was hoping this would knock me out to a point where I didn't care if I lived or died. But the whiskey didn't help much, and throughout the flight I was glued to my seat, all white knuckles and cold sweat. It was a huge relief to land in Stockholm eight hours later.

A friend picked me up at the airport and took me to Helga

who lived in a suburb of Stockholm. Her rose-colored house had not changed and the garden was wild and overgrown as usual. Helga, now eighty years old, was in bed and looked pitiful—thinner and paler than I had ever seen her. A few weeks earlier she had fallen and hurt herself badly, and had withered away since then. She also had a weak heart. I was shocked to see her and prayed she would not die. A life without Helga seemed impossible, and I wept at the very thought of losing her.

For several weeks I was her full time nurse, housekeeper and secretary. I had come armed with herbs and vitamins and Doctor Richard Schulze's "Handbook for Patients." Schulze is a famous personality in American alternative medicine. Some of the things he advocates are detoxification and internal cleanses of the body, vegetarian food, prayer, laughter and love. He also says: "Throw out or give away one third of everything you own. Bury your possessions before they bury you." This was particularly applicable to Helga as she had an unbelievable amount of junk in her house. In the cabinets were hundreds of worn out sheets, pillowcases, towels and tablecloths she had inherited from her parents. She had saved big boxes of unimportant letters and magazines from the 1970s to present time. The kitchen was full of cracked cups and pots without handles, and in her closet were dozens of garments she hadn't worn for decades. Her studio, in a separate building next to her house, was full of fabulous paintings and sculptures, but had not been cleaned for years.

I cooked for Helga and made nutritional drinks. She didn't think much of my cooking, but liked the drinks. We gave away at least a third of her clothes, books, linen and kitchenware. I stood by her bed holding up the various items and she said yes or no to trashing them. If she hesitated more than five seconds about some item, it would go in the trash bag. Helga was gleeful, nervous and delighted all at once. I honestly believe this contributed to her recovery.

Every part of her house and studio was combed through. In the end we had filled a whole container with discarded things, and had to hire a guy to haul it away. Before that my cousins and a few neighbors had been there to pick up whatever they could use. In the end her house and studio were pleasantly organized and orderly.

When Helga got better we had some good talks. She told me how terribly guilty she still felt about having abandoned me when I was a child. I answered, as always, that she had already made amends for this, and that I had completely forgiven her.

(A few years later I started to write this book. I wrote two versions, an English and a Swedish. Since I had lived abroad for so long and my Swedish was getting rusty, Helga offered to edit and correct my Swedish manuscript. I sent her version after version of my chapters. The first time she read the chapters about my childhood she wept copiously. Then she corrected my errors and I sent her the next version. This time she cried again but not as much. The third time she did not cry at all, and seemed to finally have forgiven herself for what occurred when I was young. In this way the book became a therapy for Helga as well as for me.)

We also talked about death. She wrote her will and planned her funeral. She had specific wishes for who should talk and what music should be played. Since we both believed in rebirth, I asked her where she wanted to be next lifetime. She said she wanted to be near me, and I told her I would be on the lookout for suitable parents for her, when that time came.

Another good experience in Stockholm was to spend some time with my half-sister Nadja. She was born to Peter and Gunilla in 1972, when Peter was fifty-six years old. While Nadja was growing up I was away from Sweden most of the time, and I also had strained relations with Peter and Gunilla. Therefore I did not see much of Nadja. (I saw even less of my half-brother Paul and stepbrother Micke.)

Nadja was now grown up and a successful actress at the Royal Dramatic Theatre in Stockholm. She was one of Ingmar Bergman's favorite actresses, and worked with him on stage, movies and TV.

This was the first time Nadja and I met as two adults. We talked a long time about our work and our family, especially about Peter. For Nadja he had been a good father, and she still missed him very much. She questioned me about Mutti and Daddy who had died long before she was born, and about our aunt Irene, whom she had only met once and hardly remembered. This was odd, since Alingsås is only a few hours by train from Stockholm. I told her to visit Irene before it was too late.

The day we met, Nadja also found out she was pregnant with her first child. The news shocked her so much that she fainted! Thyra, her daughter with actor Pontus Gustafsson, was born in February 1998.

We all had feared that Helga was dying, but she recovered fully within a few weeks. When she was back in her studio, painting, it was time for me to return to Florida.

THE FREIGHTER

When I cross the Atlantic, I normally go with the Queen Elizabeth II, a huge and quite luxurious passenger ship. But all affordable tickets on the QE II were sold out in July 1997, and I decided to go home on a freighter. It wasn't easy to find a suitable cargo ship, but I finally located one that was going from Valencia in eastern Spain, to Charleston, South Carolina.

I took the train from Stockholm to Geneva to see the Franceschetti family, old friends who live in a castle in the mountains. The train ride through Switzerland was spectacular as always. There is so much to see when you travel through Europe—medieval cities, picturesque villages, high mountains, green pastures and grazing animals. There are no vast unpopulated areas like in some parts of America.

After a day in Geneva I went on to Valencia which has a large seaport. The freighter area alone is colossal. I arrived early and walked around for a couple of hours in this unusual environment. There were endless rows of containers, and bright-colored cranes lifting them on and off the ships that lay anchored by the docks. It was a new world for me.

Finally my ship, the "Adriana," came in and I could go aboard. The travel agent had told me there would be several passengers, but I now found out I was the only one, and the only woman on board! This was an unpleasant surprise.

Compared to the QE II this was a small and austere kind of vessel. It carried hundreds of containers and had only a narrow strip for people to move around in. But I had a large, comfortable cabin on the upper deck, with a good size bath, and two portholes with a view of the sea. (On the QE II, the affordable cabins are tiny, and way below sea level.) There were a couple of lawn chairs on deck, and a miniscule swimming pool that was filled daily with fresh seawater.

I ate with the captain and officers in the modest dining room. The food was very simple. There was a lounge with a VCR, a few bad movies, and worse paperbacks. I now bitterly missed the QE II with its large library, interesting activities, several first class restaurants, shops, cinema and even a small synagogue. And above all, passengers! On the QE II I have met some fascinating people. All I could do on Adriana was to read, and I was glad I had brought my own books.

We sailed past the Rock of Gibraltar to the small town of Algeciras at the southernmost point of Spain. This is the last port in Europe, and here we spent a day loading more containers. I went ashore for a few hours, exploring this quaint little town, which had a strong Moorish influence. There was a market where swarthy merchants sold colorful Arabic clothing, handmade suitcases, fruit, spices and live birds. It smelled of saffron and leather goods. Some shops sold gorgeous fabrics, brocades and laces that I had never seen in Europe or America, and I bought several kinds to use in my appliqués.

Then we left Europe, through the Strait of Gibraltar. We were so close to the North African coast that I could see the Moroccan cities of Ceuta and Tangier glitter like jewels in the twilight. Soon we were on the open sea, where we would spend the next seven days.

Gradually I got to know most of the crew. The captain was German, a cold and cynical man in his sixties. He was clearly displeased about having me on board. "The greedy owner of the ship is trying to make extra money by taking passengers," he said. He also made derogatory comments about Blacks and Jews, even though I told him I did not appreciate such comments, and that I was half Jewish myself.

Two of the three officers were Croatians. They spoke bad English but were nice, and talked to me about their country, its problems and politics. One of the officers kept asking me, politely but persistently, to spend the nights with him in his cabin. I declined, explaining that I was married. He was amazed and exclaimed: "But husband far away! No tell husband!" I thought this was hilarious and laughed for several minutes, hurting his feelings. I tried to describe my moral codes, but he couldn't understand them.

There were eighteen crewmembers altogether, and the remaining fifteen were from the Philippines. They were delightful people, always friendly, laughing and joking. In the evenings they sang and played instruments. I had never met any Filipinos before, but now I made many friends and got much information about their islands. I asked them how they were all able to be so cheerful and nice. They said they were brought up that way by their parents; it was simply their way of life. They were also deeply religious Catholics.

Gabriel, the first officer, told me about Philippine faith healing. In the 1980s I had read about this and seen photos, but didn't know what to think of it. Gabriel said that on the islands there were certain saint-like people who perform operations with their bare hands, without instruments, on seriously ill patients. The healers remove tumors and repair organs, and leave no scars. There is no pain and the patient is awake all the time. Miracles are performed, like restoration of sight in the blind. It had been documented many times on photos and video. Gabriel knew one of the healers and had been present at some of the operations.

It was calm and sunny on the Atlantic for the first six days. On the last day, only a few hours away from our destination in Charleston, I was sitting on deck, reading as usual. At one point, when I happened to look up, I saw a huge dark pillar-like shape at the horizon. I ran up to the bridge, where I found the captain and two officers looking at this thing with binoculars. They told me it was a twister, a tornado. It was coming directly at us. My knees started to wobble and I felt nauseous. The captain muttered: "If this thing hits us we've had it." They steered the ship away from it at maximum speed, and we managed to just avoid it. If that twister had hit us, thousands of tons of water would have been thrown over us, and we probably would have keeled over. This was the hurricane season. I decided to never again travel on this part of the Atlantic in the summer or autumn.

In the evening we finally sailed into Charleston. When we were close to the harbor, I discerned a small white car, and a person waving. Through binoculars I could see it was Stu! He had been driving all the way from Florida to pick me up—a nine-hour trip. I didn't know he was coming. Never in my life had I been so happy to see someone.

WASHINGTON D.C.

In 1999 Stu and I were among the people who thought there might be computer crashes and widespread problems the following year—the year 2000, or Y2K. We wanted to do whatever we could to prevent such problems, and became part of a local grass-roots group—Citizens for a Stable Community (CSC). It had been established by our friend Judy Hadley.

The main objective of the group was to make sure our city and county, electric suppliers, banks and other institutions would be Y2K compliant in time, meaning that all their systems would be converted and ready. Some of them were far behind. Stu created a web site for us, where we described our plans and activities.

For almost a year Judy gave weekly briefings at the local Public Library, and I helped organize meetings and seminars around Pinellas County. We had action plans for possible emergencies, and calmed individuals who were scared and upset about the alarming Y2K articles in newspapers and magazines.

A lot of people attended these events, and we cooperated with local government officials and leaders of many churches. I found that there were about *seven hundred* churches, synagogues, mosques, temples and other religious groups in our county, although it had less than a million permanent residents! This is an astonishing amount, compared to for example Stockholm, a European capital with more than a million inhabitants and only two hundred thirty religious congregations. I realized that most Americans belong to a church of some kind, which is not the case in Sweden.

Somehow the CSC came to the attention of the White House in Washington D.C. They must had seen our web site, or heard about us through our city or county.

One day Judy got a call from Janet Abrams, John Koskinen's assistant. Koskinen was the man President Clinton had appointed to organize all White House Y2K programs. He was called the "Y2K Czar" and frequently appeared on national TV.

Judy first thought it was a joke when Janet said she was calling from the White House. But Janet had studied hundreds of grass-root Y2K groups in America, and had chosen us as one of the three best. Janet wanted Judy to speak at a White House press conference on May 24th, 1999, in the prestigious National Press Club.

We were thrilled. Judy, her mother Mardy, who was also active in the group, and I went to Washington. Mardy would videotape and I would take photos.

I spent the first afternoon walking through the city, admiring the architecture. The next morning we went to the National Press Club which was situated in a large building near the White House. Many journalists and TV crews from CNN and other networks were already there. Janet Abrams welcomed us, treating us (especially Judy) as VIPs, and introduced us to John Koskinen and several congressmen and other celebrities.

It struck me how immaculate and elegant these people looked. All the men, even twenty-year-old boys, wore three piece suits and silk ties. The women had tailor-made outfits, high heel shoes of the latest fashion, perfect hair cuts and make-up. I felt hopelessly sloppy and unfashionable, although I was wearing my best skirt and jacket.

In Sweden I had been to many events where the Prime Minister or other government officials were present. Birgitta Dahl, the Speaker of the House of the Swedish Parliament, was a close friend of Helga's. How different they are from the Americans! The Swedes are natural and informal. In Washington the government people seemed to take themselves very seriously. They looked and acted as though they were performing in a show, even when no cameras were rolling.

I remembered a story Birgitta told us at a party in Stockholm in 1997. She said she had recently visited a music store in Washington D.C., looking for old records. As usual, she was casually dressed and wore no make up. She got into a conversation with the sales people, who noticed she was a foreigner and asked what she was doing in D.C. She told them she was going to a conference, and that her job in Sweden was equivalent to Newt Gingrich's in the U.S. They laughed and thought she was joking. No way would they believe that such a natural-looking woman could be a prominent politician.

John Koskinen opened the press conference, introducing the White House Campaign of Year 2000 Conversions. He said Y2K was a potentially serious situation that the American people needed to be aware of.

There were several distinguished speakers. Judy was the only woman among them. She gave a terrific presentation about every citizen's responsibility for the society and the planet, and got thunderous applause. I was very proud of her, and Koskinen was so impressed that he half jokingly offered her a job as his PR agent.

The White House had printed a large brochure about Y2K. In it were two whole pages with color photos about our group. It was presented as a stellar example of what individual citizens can do in their communities.

Luckily Y2K turned out to be just that "non-event" we had hoped for. I like to think that groups like ours contributed to avoiding the catastrophe.

TEXAS

Miguel and Natasha Arguello are artists and among my closest friends. For many years they lived in a small camper, a truck they had converted into a home. It had a bed, a tiny kitchenette, a bench for two persons to sit on, and a narrow closet. They parked the camper in the deserts of Utah, Colorado or Texas, and painted there full time for long periods. Sometimes they came to Florida.

My first encounter with Miguel and his art was 1993 in the New York studio where he then lived and worked. Miguel was born and raised in Madrid, and his paintings are done in the technique of the old Spanish masters, beautiful and strangely moving. Apparently realistic, they have a spiritual quality and seem to show a different world. I consider him one of the finest contemporary painters on the planet. I also met Natasha, an excellent, versatile artist in her own right.

Miguel has taught at the University of California, exhibited in many countries and is mentioned in several art books. He and Natasha are both captivating, affectionate personalities and their friends adore them.

When I met them in 1993 they were about to leave New York, to live and travel in their camper. They invited me to come out in the wilderness and paint with them. It was very tempting, but I couldn't do it then because of my other duties and activities. Now, more than seven years later, I was finally on my way to visit them in the Texas desert.

It takes about forty-eight hours to go on Amtrak, the American railway, from Florida to western Texas. I had my own little cabin, where I slept deeply, although I was normally an insomniac. The food onboard was delicious. The chef specialized in seafood and salads, and fresh fruit was always available. Over the meals I talked with a former mayor of Tallahassee (the capital of Florida) and a couple of orthopedic surgeons on their way to a convention in California. Like me, they disliked flying, and valued the train.

We stopped a few hours in New Orleans, a town where I had never been. It happened to be Mardi Gras, and there were parades and enormous crowds of people in the streets. The city was extremely dirty. You couldn't walk without stepping on cigarette butts, empty beer cans and broken carnival decorations. Many people were drunk and several teenagers lay unconscious on the sidewalks.

During the train ride through Florida, Alabama, Mississippi and Louisiana, the countryside had been flat, green and densely populated. We went by marshes, bayous, old mansions and plantations, and so it continued through eastern Texas.

On the third morning I woke up in the desert. It was a shock to suddenly be in a moon-like landscape with high brown hills and almost no flora. No people, no habitation. We were in southwestern Texas.

After some time the train stopped in Alpine, a small Wild West kind of town, where the Arguellos picked me up. Miguel looked suntanned and healthy. As usual his hair came down to his shoulders and he wore several rows of beads around his neck. Natasha, who is a dark Mexican beauty, was six months pregnant with their first child.

They had borrowed an old jeep and we now drove for two hours into the real desert and high mountains. Our destination was Terlingua, by the Big Bend National Park and Mexican border. The landscape was stunning. Now I understood that "desert" is not necessarily just sand, but can be dry mountains without trees. There was low shrubbery and cactus, and a carpet of miniscule flowers in vivid colors— turquoise, lemon-yellow, pink and magenta.

Terlingua is a village spread out over many miles. The name means "three languages," as it used to be populated by three peoples: Mexicans, Indians and Anglo-Saxons. It probably had a violent past, and on a poster I read: "There is nothing that cannot be solved by the use of high explosives." One part of the village was a "ghost town," which consisted solely of ruins and burnt-out cars.

On the main street was a motel, a tiny post office, a gas station that sold exceedingly expensive gasoline, a couple of odd and exotic restaurants, and a few small stores.

The air was dry and the temperature changed quickly from ice cold to scorching hot. Most people I saw were deeply tanned and wrinkled from the sun and wind.

Miguel's camper was parked on a mountain plateau, far away from other habitation. To get there we drove up narrow and dangerous-looking paths along the side of the mountain. I was scared, and still don't know how they were able to get the jeep, let alone the camper, up and down those serpentine paths. I asked Natasha how she did it and she said: "You have to *be* the car."

From the plateau you could see miles of desert and mountains in all directions. The closest mountains were the color of burnt sienna and olive green, and the faraway ones looked blue and grey. There was complete silence up there, a kind of silence that does not exist in cities or even in the countryside. No insects were humming, no birds chirping.

Miguel had an easel set up near the camper and was working daily on a large painting of the mountains. Natasha used an old church down in Terlingua as her studio. There she painted her still lifes, using animal skulls she had found in the desert, or statues of the Virgin of Guadalupe, Mexico's patron saint. The church had been abandoned for decades and all its windows were broken. Swallows had built nests in opposite corners of the ceiling, and flew between the nests and sang all day long while Natasha painted.

The first night I slept in a tent next to the camper. Being a city person and never having camped before, this was a new experience. I was afraid of mountain lions and coyotes (we saw two of them very near the camper) and it was hard to have no toilet, shower or hot water.

It was strange to sleep under the stars in the total silence, and watch the spectacular sunrise over the mountains in the morning. I felt like a part of nature, a part of eternity. Still, I moved to the motel the next day.

The Arguellos had a dog named Carmelito. He was a stray they had found in the desert a few years earlier, and he traveled with them wherever they went. Carmelito was the luckiest animal I had ever met. Miguel and Natasha gave him an abundance of affection and attention and treated him like a family member. His job was to protect the Arguellos, and he took it very seriously, keeping coyotes and other intruders at bay. He was never on a leash, had unlimited space to run around in, and even had a dog girlfriend, Chapolina, who lived nearby.

It truly warmed my heart to see an animal so loved and cared for. Somehow it is a small compensation for the many abused and neglected animals in the world. Like Helga, I feel strongly for all animals, wild and tame, big and small.

Miguel and Natasha treated each other with exceptional tenderness and patience. They treated me (and probably all their friends) with the same kindness. We had many long, profound and honest talks about art and life. The Arguellos think for themselves and never repeat clichés they have heard from others. There is no social chit-chat with them.

We met some of their friends and other people who lived in Terlingua. These people were very poor in the material sense. They lived primitively in old, broken down trailers or in simple houses they had built themselves from mud. Some did not have electricity. One couple had disconnected completely from the U.S. society. Jack and Bonnie were well-educated people who years ago had lived normal American lives with steady jobs and salaries. One day they bailed out and moved to the desert. Now they lived in an old bus, on top of a mountain, with no address. They had two goats that gave them milk and cheese, and a small plot where they grew organic vegetables. Their only income was from occasional jobs they did for friends. I had never seen anyone voluntarily live like that in the Western world, but they seemed quite serene and satisfied.

Mexico is just a short boat ride across the river, and there we went one afternoon. This is the Rio Grande, which runs all the way from Colorado to the Gulf of Mexico, but it is narrow and shallow in many places. Usually the poverty is even greater on the Mexican side, but we visited a family that was comparatively well off. They had a modest farm with donkeys, goats and ostriches, and a rundown restaurant with two broken tables and three chairs.

We spent a whole day in the National Park. This is a 1,250-square-mile area of hills and high mountains along the Rio Grande. (Compare to Pinellas and Hillsborough counties in Florida, which together are roughly the same size.) There are 234 miles of river within the boundaries of the park, and endless roads and paths. Here you can drive for hours without seeing any humans. Cactuses were blooming in flaming red and yellow, and tall bamboo grass stood by the water. We walked in the hills, climbed the mountains, and waded across the river. It was the most formidable, awe-inspiring landscape I have ever seen. I understood why Miguel and Natasha kept coming back to this place, and I too felt an urge to paint.

After a few days, which seemed like weeks because of all the new experiences, I had to leave. The Arguellos took me back to Alpine, where I got on a bus to Fort Stockton. I was going to San Antonio, on my way back to Florida, and this was the only route. The bus was full of Mexicans and the radio played loud Mexican pop music. Certain phrases were repeated many times, like "mi pobre madre," "esperanza" and "tristeza." This gave me an idea of the difference between the American and the Mexican cultures. What American pop singer would sing about his poor mother?

In Fort Stockton I changed to a Greyhound bus, this time packed with mostly Americans. Some of them appeared to be drug addicts or homeless people, ragged and scary looking. I sat next to a youngish man with wild eyes, tattoos all over his arms and half of his teeth missing. Surprisingly, he turned out to be the sweetest person, helpful and eager to talk.

Eventually we reached San Antonio in southern Texas. Here I was met by my dear old friends John and Jennifer Pantermuehl. We spent the first evening in the "River Walk" area in the center of town. It reminded me of Venice, Italy.

John's family owns a ranch with hundreds of goats, horses and other animals, near San Antonio. The family has lived there for generations. It is a German heritage area and all the villages, streets and stores have German names.

I stayed with John and Jennifer for two days. Like the

Arguellos they are warm, spiritual people, and we had long talks about God and religion and the most basic issues of our lives.

Once again it struck me how many wonderful, loving friends I have all over the world, and I was overwhelmed with gratitude. Every one of them is a gift and a blessing.

After San Antonio I was back on the Greyhound. It took twenty-seven backbreaking hours to return to Florida. The bus stopped in a dozen shabby little stations, throughout the day and night. In many of these stations the passengers had to get up and leave the bus for twenty minutes or so, even when we were dead tired or asleep. The restaurants at the bus stops served only junk food. I do not recommend the bus for overnight trips. The train would be so much better, but Amtrak does not have the frequent service we are used to in Europe. It only passes through Texas three times a week, and stops in San Antonio at the ungodly hour of 3:00 a.m.

My back was sore for days after the Greyhound trip, but that did not change the joy and inspiration I had received from the journey. I felt as though I had been away for months, and in another universe.

CALIFORNIA

My grandfather Eugen Weiss (Daddy) had two sisters, Aranka and Malvine, and a brother, Edmund. They were born in Hungary and then lived in Austria and Germany. In the mid 1930s, Daddy and two of his siblings understood that they had to leave their countries, and started to organize their emigration. Daddy moved to Sweden with my grandmother (Mutti) and their children Peter, Irene and Alexander.

Daddy's sister Aranka Ettinger went to England with her husband and son. His brother Edmund Weisz (who had kept the original spelling of the family name) ended up in America. His sister Malvine was the only sibling who did not escape. Subsequently she and her husband were deported by the Nazis and killed in Auschwitz.

Edmund, his wife Else and their daughter Lisa arrived in San Francisco in January 1940. Lisa was six years old, and has since then lived all her life in California. Edmund died in 1950, and Lisa lost contact with her relatives in Europe.

In the 1980s, Peter's brother Alexander managed to locate Lisa, and they started a correspondence. In 1998 Lisa and her husband, Heinz Gewing, visited Irene in Sweden. Lisa never corresponded with Peter, but read some of his books, the ones she could find in English, as her German had become too rusty.

Irene had told me about the Gewings, and I also wanted to meet them. But it did not happen, mostly because I don't fly and all my trips therefore are long and expensive.

After I moved to America I got in touch with Lisa by email and letters. When Irene died in May 2001, Lisa and I decided we had to meet, because one never knows how much time one has left.

Therefore I went to California in early August 2001. I was looking forward to seeing the Gewings, and also Amnon Levy, my old friend from kibbutz Givat Chaim. He lived in Palo Alto near San Francisco and was glad I would visit. We had not seen each other for sixteen years.

The trip to California was an adventure in itself. I took the northern route this time, through Chicago, in order to see new parts of America. Since there are no trains from Florida to Chicago, I had to take the Greyhound again, a twenty-five hour journey. In spite of the uncomfortable seat it was exciting to travel through states I had never seen before.

The road to Atlanta was flat and boring, but thereafter it became hilly and interesting. Soon we were in the Smoky Mountains, which were covered with dense, deciduous forests. Wide rivers ran between the high hills.

Some of the passengers boarding in Tennessee seemed to have mental and physical problems and looked odd, like the persons I had seen in the movie *Deliverance* with Burt Reynolds and Jon Voight in the 1970s. Later I found out that *Deliverance* had actually been filmed in these areas.

The landscape in Kentucky and Indiana reminded me of the Swedish countryside. There were even birch trees and red cottages like in Sweden. I also saw Amish people, who still lived like they did hundreds of years ago, without electricity, cars and other modern amenities. The men wore black clothes and large hats and the women dressed like they did in the 1800s. I saw them stroll in the streets, and ride in carriages drawn by horses.

We were given a new bus driver every four hours or so. The first driver, in Florida, was relaxed and friendly, but the further north we went, the angrier were the drivers. On the last leg of the journey, from Indianapolis to Chicago, our driver was a furious young black man. The first thing he did when he arrived was to scream at the passengers for several minutes. Although it was quiet and peaceful on the bus, he threatened to immediately throw off anyone who dared to smoke, drink alcohol, play music or listen to the radio. He said he would call the police and send the passengers to jail. I wondered what was normally going on in these buses.

Outside Chicago were dirty factories with high chimneys, smoke and flames, but the city itself was clean and orderly. I didn't even see any homeless people around. The skyscrapers were as high as in New York, and there were plenty of coffee houses, restaurants and shops. Traffic was dense and the streets were full of pedestrians. But the atmosphere was not at all like in New York, a city I know fairly well. Chicago was founded by Swedes, Germans and Poles, while New York is mostly inhabited by Italians, Jews and Irish. I could feel the difference. Chicago seemed calmer, cleaner and more conservative, but personally I prefer New York.

I arrived in Chicago in the evening and spent the night in a simple hotel in the center of town. The next morning I met a friend who lives near Chicago. He invited me for lunch in a restaurant which turned out to be on the ninety-sixth floor in the second tallest building in Chicago! It was called the John Hancock Center and was actually one of the highest structures in the world.

Since I have a fear of heights, I nearly panicked in the elevator when I realized how high we were going. But it was too late to protest, and I forced myself to keep calm. We were given a table by the window, from where we could see all of Chicago and the boundless Lake Michigan, but that was more than I could handle. I asked if we could move further into the room, and we found another table. The food was delicious and the conversation enjoyable, but I was very relieved when we were back on the ground floor.

There is a daily direct train from Chicago to San Francisco, and I boarded this train in the afternoon. The journey, which was supposed to take fifty hours, is considered one of the most scenic in America. My ticket included a private cabin, and three meals a day in the dining car. We traveled through Illinois, Iowa, Nebraska—states I had never seen. They were sparsely populated and we passed miles and miles of rivers, fields and forests.

After Denver, Colorado, the landscape suddenly started to change. Now we were in the Rocky Mountains, which looked a bit like the Alps in central Europe. But in Europe the trains go between the mountains and through tunnels. Here the train climbed up and up, and to my dismay we were soon at an elevation of thousands of feet! My ears hurt, I became nauseous, and was aghast when I looked out the windows. The train meandered on narrow shelves along practically vertical mountain sides. There were only a few inches between the rail and the abyss, and no fences or other security measures. If we had derailed, we would have plunged straight to the bottom of the chasm. I recalled with horror the many stories about derailing Amtrak trains I had read in the papers. A fellow passenger told me there were remains of old trains at the bottom of some canyons. These had fallen down long ago and it was too difficult and expensive to move them, so they were still there...

Anyhow, the view was sublime. Sky-high mountains capped with snow, dense spruce forests, and azure blue lakes in the valleys below. The air was clear and pure.

Eventually we were back on lower ground and traveled along the Colorado River. There the water was turquoise and the vegetation luxuriant with many kinds of trees and flowers. People were camping and hiking by the banks, and rowing canoes on the river. I wished I could step off the train and stay in Colorado.

In the dining car we always shared tables with other people since space was limited. Sometimes I sat with a nice young Catholic man in training to become a priest, sometimes with a woman who published books for the Getty Museum in Los Angeles.

Sometimes I was placed next to a slightly obese man with thin auburn hair named Kevin. He and his wife were on their way to Sacramento, California. Kevin was constantly quoting the Bible and talked only about Jesus. He told the others at the table that Jesus was the only salvation and that we would burn in hell if we didn't open our hearts to receive Him. "Praise the Lord" he added at the end of almost every sentence. It was impossible to make him change the subject. His wife sat silently, making no comments.

I have always been uncomfortable around religious fanatics, regardless of denomination. In the U.S. I have run into quite a few of them. I always wonder how they can all be so sure they are the only ones who know the truth. How they can blindly believe in something just because it is written in a book. Whenever I saw Kevin in the dining car, I tried to quickly grab a table as far as possible away from him.

To my regret I missed Salt Lake City, as we passed Utah during the night. The next day we went across endless miles of the Nevada desert. We stopped in Reno, a small town that looked oddly artificial. From the train I saw a large number of casinos and bars and very few other buildings.

After Reno we were in the next mountain range, the Sierra Nevada. Once again the train crept up thousands of feet, but much slower than earlier. When I asked the conductor why we were going so slowly, he said there had just been an earthquake in the mountains! Therefore they had a small car running in front of the train, to check if the rails had been damaged. What would they have done if there *had* been damage? Backed all the way down to Reno?

The next day I read in the paper about the earthquake which had been 5.5 on the Richter scale. I don't understand how they dared to take the train up in the mountains immediately after such a strong quake.

Still, I had to laugh at myself and my fear of heights. It was comical how I always managed to get into situations that terrified me.

Finally, five hours late, we arrived in Emeryville near San Francisco. Lisa and Heinz Gewing met me at the station and gave me a warm welcome. They were in their mid- or late sixties, but healthy and youthful. Both had thick white hair, were tanned and casually dressed. I remembered how Mutti and Daddy had looked when they were the same age—they had been *old*. But Heinz and Lisa were young. Heinz was tall, Lisa petite with big brown eyes. In her face I seemed to trace some of the features I had seen in Daddy and Peter and maybe in myself.

Heinz Gewing was born in Austria, like Lisa, but their families had not known each other there. In 1938, when the Weisz family left Austria, the Gewings fled to Shanghai, where there was a small Jewish community. After the war they continued to San Francisco. Heinz' twin brother soon got tired of America and immigrated to Israel, where he still lives on a kibbutz. Heinz stayed in California, learned to speak flawless English, but still had a slight Austrian accent. Lisa and Heinz met as teenagers in the Zionist youth movement Hashomer Hatzair. They were both educated at the Berkeley University, worked many years, and were now retired.

They married young and had been married forty-seven years. Heinz, who has a good sense of humor, said the first forty-seven years of a marriage are usually the most difficult. They have two daughters and two teenage grandchildren and

I met them all. Jenny, the older daughter, was interested in the Weisz family and very nice and easy to talk to.

Lisa, Heinz and Jenny spent days giving me the grand tour of San Francisco, Oakland, Berkeley and surrounding areas. We were in art galleries, museums and stores, on the beach and in Chinatown. One day we walked in Muir Woods, where the Redwood trees are among the highest in the world. In a park above the Golden Gate Bridge we saw an outstanding Holocaust Memorial—an assembly of many sculptures depicting a concentration camp.

The Castro district was mostly populated by gays and there were hundreds of colorful flags showing that the houses or shops were run by gays. Men walked hand in hand in the streets. The Haight-Ashbury district still had remnants of the Flower Power culture that blossomed there in the 1970s. In the streets I saw hippies with long hair and flowing robes (like I used to wear myself), and there were psychedelic frescos on the walls.

In the Mission district, which is famous for its murals, we saw at least fifty huge images in the streets. They were mostly social and political protest paintings, made by Latino artists. One of them showed South American mothers holding photographs of their vanished children. There were also gigantic portraits of Monsignor Oscar Romero, Frida Kahlo, Diego Rivera and other greats, pictures of exploited farmers, and of women and children being executed by soldiers with impassive faces.

Many of the streets in San Francisco were so steep that I couldn't fathom how the trams and cars could get up and down on them. Jenny lived on a high hill, and I refused to drive up some of the extremely steep streets that led to her house. Jenny understood and took an alternate route for me.

In a Berkeley bookstore I was surprised to find two recently published plays by Peter. I didn't know his books were being printed again, twenty years after his death, in English.

Heinz, Lisa and Jenny treated me with tremendous hospitality and generosity, as though I was their own daughter or sister. After four days with them I felt like I had known them for years. I suddenly had a brand-new family, both emotionally and biologically, and it gave me a feeling of gratitude and security. In a roundabout way I felt I had reconnected with Daddy and Peter.

On the fifth day Amnon Levy picked me up and took me to his house which was about an hour's drive from Oakland. Amnon is also part of my "family" and it was a pleasure to see him again. His parents Ruth and Aaron "adopted" me when I was in Givat Chaim in the early 1960s. I befriended Amnon and his brother Rani, and have kept in touch with the Levys for decades. Amnon and I talk on the phone every year, but I hadn't seen him since 1985.

After having fought two wars in Israel, 1967 and 1973, Amnon wanted to pursue his profession as an architect. He ended up leaving both the kibbutz and Israel, and moving to America with his wife Noah and their children. In California there were better possibilities and challenges for an architect, especially for a visionary one like Amnon. He showed me several exquisite homes and apartment complexes he had designed and built in the Palo Alto area.

Noah had left him a few years earlier and Amnon now lived alone. We visited Uri, their son, who was married and lived near Amnon. There is a certain quality I saw in Ruth Levy and both her sons, which I also recognized in Uri now that I met him as an adult. Something genuine, an honesty and purity of spirit which moved me very much.

We talked non-stop for two days. Amnon had changed greatly since I last saw him. He was more mellow, open and easy to talk to—maybe because he was now meditating and doing yoga. I got closer to him than ever before. When talking about our youth in Givat Chaim, I described my admiration for the young people in the kibbutz, and for its general system. The children seemed so proud, brave and strong—just the opposite of how I had been myself at that time.

But Amnon gave me a totally different viewpoint on this. He said the youth of the kibbutz were often emotional cripples. Since early childhood they had lived alone in their own homes, not with their parents. While I had always believed this was a good system, Amnon described the fear he and many other children felt when they were left alone in the pitch-black night. There was a guard patrolling the area, but no adult was in the house with them. The teacher or housemother only arrived in the morning.

The parents forced themselves to withhold their love, as they did not want to "spoil" the children. Amnon knew that Ruth and Aaron loved him, but this was never expressed in words, and there was very little physical affection. He was brought up by his parents and the whole kibbutz to be a strong, disciplined soldier who could defend the country. He learned to suppress all emotions and not to cry when his friends were killed in battle. It took many years before he was able to contact his own feelings, until he could improve his relationships with his own children, and open up to other people. I was shocked to hear all this. My romantic ideas about the kibbutz were largely shattered.

We looked at old photo albums Amnon had received after Ruth's death. There were pictures of Ruth and Aaron as young pioneers in Palestine. Of Amnon and Rani as babies. Wedding pictures of Amnon and Noah, Rani and Tova. Amnon's children, Rani's children. I saw recent photos as well, of Amnon's first grandchild. My friendship with the Levys has spanned over four generations and I feel a strong bond with them.

There were also snapshots from the 1980s, when Ruth visited her original home town in Germany. Here Ruth was standing by the house her parents had owned, from which they had been deported and murdered by the Nazis. Ruth had talked with the current owner, mentioning that this was once her family's house. The new owner insisted he had bought the house legally and was not interested in Ruth's story.

For some reason Ruth made no attempt to obtain redress then, while there was still a chance. I guess the visit to her home town had such an upsetting and depressing effect on her that she just wanted to forget about it and have nothing more to do with Germany.

We also went through a book about Givat Chaim that had been published for the 40th anniversary of the kibbutz. The last part of the book consisted of page after page of photos of young men. These were the members who had been killed in Israel's various wars. Among them was our friend Ofer Feniger, who had fallen in Jerusalem at age twenty-four, and whose death had such a profound impact on me.

It was hard to part from Amnon. I knew it would be a long time until I would see him again, and I had to fight back the tears.

The trip back to Florida took several days; the southern route this time. First I went to Los Angeles, crossing a new range of mountains, and passing orange groves, palm trees and cypresses. The train stopped in small towns like Modesto and Bakersfield.

I spent a day in Los Angeles, with Arnie Alpert, another dear friend and a highly unusual person. He is about my age, but still looks exactly as he did when I first met him in 1969. He is a playful, Peter Pan kind of being. Arnie did not do any of the "normal" things that are expected from men in our society. While he loves women and children, he never married or had kids of his own. Instead of getting trained in a profession, he worked in many different fields. It never occurred to him to save money for his retirement, or to buy a home or condominium. He shares a house with some friends. Outside his room he has created a most amazing, jungle-like flower garden.

In the early 1990s Arnie suddenly decided to become a professional extra and actor in movies, and this had been his job ever since. He regularly sends me photos of himself in role portraits, and I have a whole collection of these. Being Jewish, he particularly enjoys giving me pictures of himself as a Vatican priest or an Arab Sheik. He knows they make me laugh. But most often he is cast as police officers, South American gangsters or Italian Mafia members.

After Los Angeles I continued on my way home through the stupendous deserts of Arizona and New Mexico, through Texas and the southern states. When not staring out the window, I read an absorbing book by Chaim Potok, one of my favorite authors. The title is *The Gates of November*, published in 1996. It is the true story of the Slepak family, Jewish dissidents and refuseniks in the old Soviet Union. Potok's first meeting with the Slepaks in Moscow 1985 was similar to my own meeting with refuseniks in Leningrad 1984. In his description of Jewish history in Russia and Asia, Potok mentions the community in Shanghai, where Heinz Gewing lived during World War II. It was the ideal book to read at that time, and I felt that many loose ends were being tied together.

On the train through California I had been sitting next to a transvestite. He was a slim white man in his late forties. His hair was short; he wore a pink lace hat, and large earrings. Eyes and lips were skillfully painted, and there was a slight 5 o'clock shadow on his chin. He wore a T-shirt and shorts, pantyhose and ladies' shoes. His nails were brightly lacquered.

I had never before met a transvestite, and struck up a conversation with him. His name was Nicky and he was a factory worker from Baltimore, Maryland. He had been saving money for years to make this trip to California. Above all he had wanted to visit the Castro district in San Francisco, where so many gays live. Nicky described the chills that went up his spine when he first saw all the flags symbolizing a gay culture. He wanted to find someone to marry, but the gay men he met didn't like transvestites. I asked him why he then dressed as a woman anyway. Nicky replied that he had had a compulsion to wear women's clothes, as long as he could remember. He kept trying to control the urge, but eventually could no longer suppress it. Now he didn't care anymore what people thought about him. At work he had to dress as a man, but in his free time he always wore women's clothes. He had been born into the wrong body, and said he would like to have a sex change operation. But those cost at least $30.000, which he could not afford.

Nicky was a tragic figure. I felt ashamed that I had been prejudiced against him when I first saw him, and that I had thought he looked ridiculous. Even the oddest-looking people, against whom one has the worst prejudices, are often nice and kind when you get to know them. I promised myself to be less prejudiced in the future. I remembered a decision I had made three decades ago: to learn to love all people. To stop judging them, to love them even though it's hard, and in spite of all their faults. When I have truly learnt this, perhaps my own faults will vanish.

NEW YORK

2001 was my year of connecting up with old friends and new relatives. It was an odyssey crisscrossing America.

I had planned to visit Tana Ross, Bill Tatum and Brenda Dixon in New York in September 2001. Tana is the Swedish girl from Givat Chaim, Bill and Brenda are the African-Americans I met in the 1960s. We were in the process of finding a date that would suit us all.

On the 11th of September we still had not agreed on a date. In the morning I was at home, working on my computer as usual. Around 9:20 a.m. Stu called from his office and told me to turn on the TV. On CNN, I saw the horrific events in New York and Washington that everyone now is familiar with.

My friends lived in Manhattan, not far from the World Trade Center. I tried to call them, but all the phone lines to New York were dead. Around 9:45 a.m. I managed to contact Helga in Sweden, telling her not to worry about me. I knew she would worry although New York is far from Florida. After that I couldn't get through to any other cities in Europe or America. I emailed Tana and Bill but there were no replies.

Stu closed his office and came home to sit by the TV with me. The events at WTC and Pentagon were played over and over. It was hard to grasp that all this was actually happening.

The next day I was finally able to reach my friends in New York and was immensely relieved to hear that they and their families were OK. But all the others? The thousands of innocents in the towers, in the Pentagon and in the airplanes? The large number of policemen and fire fighters who had perished? All the families who had lost loved ones?

A hundred people from our little town in Florida immediately took action. They rented buses and went to New York to help out as volunteers. Arriving on September 14th, they worked around the clock at Ground Zero. One of them was David, the seventeen-year-old son of one of our best friends. Later he told us how he delivered food and drinks to the rescue workers every day, massaged their tired backs and helped with anything else that was needed. He also participated in the cleanup of areas a few blocks away from Ground Zero. These streets were full of paper and office materials that had blown out of the towers at the explosions. David had been close to tears when he found personal notebooks, stamps and photographs.

The air at Ground Zero was toxic and though the volunteers wore masks, many of them got allergic reactions and breathing problems. In spite of that they kept working for days and weeks on end.

As we all know, the American people were united at that time. For a short while there were no more quarrels between political parties or between family members or neighbors. I felt stronger than ever that most Americans are good, tolerant and courageous people, who desire peace and freedom. For the first time since we came to the U.S. I felt like an American, and decided to apply for citizenship as soon as I was eligible.

My trip to New York did not materialize until the end of October, six weeks after the terror attacks. As usual I took the train, which was packed with people who no longer dared to fly. In the dining car I sat next to a biochemist from New Jersey, whose wife had forbidden him to fly since September 11th. He said he had realized that life is short and you have to make the best of it while you still have a chance. Now he was spending more time with his family and tried to be as kind and loving as possible.

When we approached New York and I looked out the window I noticed something was wrong with the skyline of the city. The two high towers were missing and it was a shock to see the change.

The Amtrak station in New York was full of policemen and security personnel. I tried to leave my suitcase at a baggage claim, but it had closed down for security reasons. The taxi stands, normally next to the station, had been moved a block away, also for safety reasons. At least fifty people were waiting for taxis.

After standing in the taxi line for forty-five minutes, I finally got a cab and went to Bill and Susan Tatum's house in the East Village in southern Manhattan. In this part of town the grocery stores, restaurants and movie theatres are open twenty-four hours a day and the streets are always crowded. Most of the people who live there seem to know each other and chat when they meet in the streets. It is like a small town, in the middle of the enormous city of New York.

Bill was a Freedom Rider in the South in the early 1960s, and has always been an active and dynamic man. After an accident a few years ago he was now in a wheel chair, hardly able to move his arms and legs. The newspaper he used to publish—one of the largest African-American papers—had been taken over by his daughter Ellie. Bill still wrote the editorials, dictating them to his secretary. In spite of all, Bill was in surprisingly good spirits, laughing, joking and discussing politics as usual.

When I arrived, Bill and Susan were watching the morning

news on TV, and I heard that New York was on "full alert" again this day. A new anthrax death had just occurred in a Manhattan hospital, and there were new threats of terrorism. I wished I had stayed in Florida.

At the breakfast table we talked about the terror acts. Bill said: "As long as there is so much poverty and suffering in the third world, the people there will hate America and will support groups that try to take revenge." This seemed to be an unusual opinion in the U.S. Most other Americans I had talked to said that religious fanaticism, not economics, was the reason for the attacks.

The Tatums' house was a half-hour walk from Ground Zero. I wanted to see it, and walked south along Broadway. On the way I passed a building that had a line of people standing in front of it. I had never seen such a long line—it stretched around the whole block. I asked a policeman what these people were waiting for, and he said they were foreigners who were trying to get a visa to stay in the U.S. After September 11th the immigration rules had become much stricter and many foreigners were now risking deportation. In front of the next building was an equally long line in the street. These were people who had lost their jobs because of the terror attacks, or were applying for disaster relief.

A few blocks from Ground Zero I began to perceive something peculiar in the air—something horrible but indefinable. When I got closer I could identify a smell of chemicals and something burning. Ground Zero was closed off, but in the distance I saw a huge gaping hole with a few blackened, distorted metal shapes that had once been buildings. It was incomprehensible and surreal that the famous towers I had been used to seeing for so many years no longer existed. Thousands of people had died here only a few weeks earlier, and somehow I could perceive their emotions. It was as though their despair and horror still lingered in the air.

It was profoundly disturbing to see Ground Zero. I will never ever forget the sight.

After a day with the Tatums I took the bus to Tana who lives in northern Manhattan. The ride took over an hour because of the traffic jams. Traveling through the city, I once again noticed the incredible diversity that makes New York so special. The subway had been closed, due to a bomb threat, and therefore the bus was packed. Among the passengers were two orthodox Jews with long beards and black hats, a couple of Russians chatting in their native tongue, several African-Americans and Latinos, some Chinese or Japanese, a businessman in a pin stripe suit and attaché case, a super-elegant model, an old woman dressed in rags and talking to herself, and a teenager with purple hair who played the harmonica. All these people, with their highly dissimilar cultures and religions, live in New York side by side in relative harmony. I felt a surge of admiration for all of them. How could someone want to murder these people?

Several years often pass between my meetings with Tana, and it was good to see her again. We talked about the kibbutz where we first had met, and compared our experiences. Our time in Givat Chaim had been intense and emotional for both of us. We laughed at some of the memories, and once again marveled and joked about the handsome young men of the kibbutz.

Tana showed me the film *Silence* which is about her own childhood in Theresienstadt, the Nazi concentration camp. It was deeply moving. I now understood Tana better than before and I admire her ability to survive physically and emotionally.

The next day I met Brenda Dixon, whom I had not seen for thirty years. She hadn't changed much—as a professional dancer and choreographer she was slim, fit and graceful. She still had the lightness of being that had drawn me to her in the 1960s. A writer as well as a dancer, she was working on her fifth book about dance. Like Tana, she was very depressed about the terror attacks and the current war in Afghanistan.

After two days with Tana I took the train back to Florida. During the long hours of the journey I had time to ponder over the events of September 11th, the threat of biological warfare, and the poverty in the third world.

I also thought about other tragedies that constantly occur in America. The worst are those involving children. Every year thousands of persons vanish in this country and two thirds of them are children. Some are eventually located, dead or alive, but many are never found. I have read that a number of these children are sold as slaves to groups that deal in child-sex, drugs and pornography. This is a fate much worse than death, for both the children and their parents who never find out what happened to them. The issues of child abuse and disappearance are among the most important in the world.

There *have* to be solutions to all these problems. We *cannot* accept that they continue and get worse.

It is not enough to put a few kidnappers and child molesters in prison. It doesn't help to bomb third world countries or execute some terrorists. War and punishment are short-lived and uncertain solutions.

If I were president of a country, I would create a forum for new ideas, methods and solutions. I would invite any individuals, organizations or groups to present their programs and statistics for social betterment and world peace. I would examine and test any new ideas that seemed workable. I know this sounds naive, but the old methods clearly do not work, so we *have* to find new ways. All true solutions have to be based on tolerance, justice and workability.

HELGA

In the spring of 2002, Helga wasn't feeling well. In February, when she turned eighty-five, there had been great festivities that left her exhausted for weeks. She spent a lot of time in bed, but in the morning hours when she still had a bit of energy, she worked, writing and painting. Despite her condition, she produced an amazing number of exquisite little water colors. I found several that were dated in June 2002, just days before her first heart attack.

On July 1st, she got severe chest pains and was rushed to the Emergency Room at the Karolinska Hospital in Stockholm. Her nieces Susanna, Veronica and Laila were at her side, and I arrived from Florida within a few days.

I was with Helga in the hospital every day. She was pale, emaciated and so weak that no long conversations were possible. But she was glad I was there. I lived alone in her rose-colored house, which was eerily empty without her. As always, the summer evenings were white and transparent. The sun descended about 11:00 p.m. and rose again two hours later.

After a couple of weeks Helga was sent home. I took care

of her, with the help of nurses who came daily. Helga was not in pain but had breathing problems and could only eat liquid food.

She talked about unfinished sculptures and other projects she wanted to do. One of her wishes was to donate some of her art to the Sundbyberg City Hall, if a permanent exhibition could be organized there. (Sundbyberg is a small town just outside Stockholm, where Helga had lived since 1976.) The donation was arranged just a few days before her death.

Helga did not want to be in a home for the aged. She was mentally clear until the end, and refused to be around senile people. But she could not manage by herself at home, even with daily visits from a nurse. We had an unsolvable problem. I could not stay in Sweden indefinitely, so I started to examine some retirement homes and hospitals. The ones I saw were not acceptable and I knew Helga would hate them.

On August 10th Helga's health deteriorated further and we took her back to the hospital. I sat by her bed every day, and my cousins came often. Other people tried to visit, but she only wanted to see her immediate family. On the 15th I was with Helga for several hours. She had been given oxygen, was able to breathe easily and was surprisingly alert.

When I asked how she was doing, she did not want to discuss her health. Instead she talked about Susanna's cat, which had been very brave and chased away a large fox that was threatening her kittens.

She also told me about a recurring dream or vision she was having. To understand this vision, one has to be familiar with Helga's art. Two of her favorite themes, throughout her life, have been horses and cows. They were connected with her childhood. She adored these animals, and painted them over and over.

Helga said: "In my vision, I am walking on a meadow. Bees

are humming and birds singing. After a while I no longer see my feet, only my footprints in the grass. Then I am floating above the ground, as though I am carried. In the far distance I see a wonderful green pasture, where incredibly beautiful horses and cows are grazing. I know I am on my way to this pasture."

In the night between the 15th and 16th I couldn't sleep. Around 3:00 a.m. I was suddenly short of breath. At 4:00 a.m. the phone rang. The doctor said: "It is about your mother." She had had a new heart attack, called for help and died within minutes. The doctor said it had been quick and she had not suffered.

An hour later I was in the hospital. Helga was stretched out on a white bed in a small private room. Her face looked young and peaceful. A nurse, who had read Helga's books and knew that Helga liked feathers, had put a feather on her bed. I wept inconsolably for a long time but could still not believe she was dead. Time stood still. Everything seemed to stop.

Helga had dreaded disability, senility or prolonged illness and I was glad she had been spared all of that.
But death is a strange thing. Even when a parent is old, even when death is almost expected, as a child one is never prepared for it. I was devastated. I felt like a lost, abandoned child, although I was a grown person. I felt I was shipwrecked and floating alone on the ocean, with no land in sight. Like a flower torn up with my roots.

Some parents love their children unconditionally. Although Helga had failed me as a child, although we had bad relations in my teens, although she could sometimes be difficult even in recent years, I knew she loved me unconditionally. During the last few decades she had been an anchor in my life. She would have taken me in and helped me had I become a criminal or drug addict or other type of misfit. She would not have hesitated to give her life for me.

I think this kind of love occurs only from parents to children. Your husband, your wife, your friends or your sons and daughters seldom love you that way. Not until now, when Helga was gone, did I fully understand what I had lost.

Not all parents love their children unconditionally. I now realized how lucky I had been, what a tremendous privilege it had been to have such a mother. And that I had her for so long.

Helga was always there to help, support and communicate. She was extremely interested in every detail of my existence, as I was in hers. We talked on the phone twice a week, and shared everything. In the winters she visited me and Stu in Florida, glad to get away from the Swedish cold. During these visits she met all my friends, and as usual got along fabulously with people half her age. Some of my friends developed personal relationships with her and corresponded with her when she was back in Sweden. She was very fond of Miguel and Natasha and even their dog Carmelito.

And she delighted in nature. She was fascinated by the events in her jungle-like garden and admired the trees for being able to create so much change and beauty all by themselves. If a plant, which had seemed to be dead, would suddenly grow new buds and flowers, she would be ecstatic.

She had a white cat, named Plumpen, who was dear to her. When the cat died in 2000 at age seventeen, both Helga and I were grief-stricken. Helga buried Plumpen in her garden, and on Plumpen's grave wild strawberries began to grow.

Even when Helga's body was old, she was a young girl in

spirit. While many older people tend to have fixed ideas, Helga never did. She remained open, tolerant, curious about everything, always willing to examine and re-examine ideas and situations. Like me, she was a spiritual person, convinced that we are all immortal beings who have lived before and will live again.

She was passionate in her goals and projects, fighting for them until the end. She made posters and postcards for Amnesty International, and spoke on national TV about Children's Rights and Animal Rights. She supported religious, cultural, social and political organizations.

Helga was a rare and brilliant artist. Her style was unmistakable, her images like no one else's, and she had a scope and versatility that few artists have. The poems are as unique and gripping as the paintings. Many of them have been published in books and magazines, but in her drawers I found superb and hilarious poems written to friends and relatives, still unpublished.

The message in her books, paintings, cartoons and posters was always cheerful, defiant and optimistic. No wonder she was so appreciated.

Here is one of Helga's poems, called *SPEAK,* in my own translation from Swedish. This poem has been used by Amnesty, and was recited in the Swedish Parliament for Crown Princess Victoria, on her twenty-first birthday. In 1986 it was quoted at Swedish Prime Minister Olof Palme's funeral. On September 19th, 2003, it was recited at the Memorial Service of Anna Lindh, the Swedish Foreign Minister who had been murdered a few days earlier. The service was televised live in the presence of royalties and top politicians from all over the world.

Speak
You who still have lips
Speak

speak to the neighbors in the hallway
speak to the people in the street
and in the underground

those who still have ears
will hear

write words on paper
on walls and on banners
carry the words through the city
high above your heads
so everyone can see

distribute leaflets
about freedom, resistance, peace,
*   solidarity and human dignity*

let the words fly like swallows
to faraway countries
guided by the stars
like doves of hope
to our sisters and brothers
in the prisons of the world
those who could not be silent

speak
you who still have lips

words can become suns
words can become rivers
words can open gates
and build bridges
words can overthrow tyrants
if enough of us
arm ourselves with words

speak speak
it is our duty
to those who spoke
while they still had lips

Many people will miss Helga. She played a large role in the lives of her friends and family members. Some of them told me it is a huge blow for them to no longer be able to talk to her.

Going through her belongings I found big boxes with letters. Some were from friends and relatives but many were from people she had never met. They thanked her for her books and art, saying she had changed or saved their lives.

In her will she asked for a happy funeral. She wanted a minister she personally knew, and specific music and speakers. Afterwards she wanted a reception in her home, with plenty of sandwiches, cake, coffee, wine and sherry.

My cousin Laila and I worked on the obituary and funeral program, which was printed on rose-colored paper, with one of Helga's joyful drawings on the cover.

Birgitta Dahl, the Speaker of the House of the Swedish Parliament, agreed to talk at the funeral. So did Maj Britt Theorin, member of the European Parliament in Brussels. The minister Madeleine Åhlstedt agreed to hold the service, and the opera singer Busk Margit Jonsson was pleased to sing. All of them were friends of Helga's.

But we were unable to find someone who could sing "Gracias a la vida" by Violeta Parra. This is a song Helga liked and which was performed at Olof Palme's funeral. Busk Margit couldn't do that one. We had given up on it, and I was already "apologizing to Helga," when out of the blue we received a call from a Cuban singer who lived in Stockholm. Her name is Maria Llerena. She said she knew Helga, and volunteered to sing "Gracias a la vida"!

About two hundred people came to the early afternoon funeral on Thursday, August 29th. Most of them wore light-colored clothing, per Helga's wishes. The white coffin was decorated not only with flowers but with feathers in many colors. (Helga often put feathers on her sculptures, to symbolize courage and freedom.)

Madeleine, Birgitta and Maj Britt each spoke beautifully about their personal memories of Helga. (Birgitta's speech was also published in Dagens Nyheter, Sweden's largest newspaper.)

Busk Margit sang a haunting tune, and when Maria sang in Spanish I could feel Helga smiling and dancing to the rhythm.

After the funeral, over a hundred people came to Helga's house. It was the last warm day of summer and many of us sat all afternoon on the grass in her large, overgrown garden. There was plenty of delicious food and drink.

People talked about Helga and were sad and happy all at once. For me it was a marvel to reunite with some of my cousins and other relatives and friends whom I had not seen for years or decades. I felt "carried" by their love, like Helga had felt carried in her dream.

The next day the colossal task of emptying and selling Helga's house began. It was tough to do. Every photograph, every little item was painful to look at. Helga was gone, and now the house, which had been my home in Sweden, would also have to go.

On the following weekend, per Helga's wishes, we made an exhibition of her art in her studio. My cousins helped me put it together. (Stu, who had arrived from Florida the day after Helga's death, had to leave again after the funeral.) The show was a success. There were so many visitors and sales that my hand was aching from writing receipts.

The Museum of Modern Art in Stockholm bought a few pieces, and the National Museum bought one of her self-portraits for their collections. The Södertälje Art Museum planned a retrospective exhibition of Helga's life and work for the spring of 2003.

Susanna, Veronica and Laila came to the house daily to support me in every conceivable way. The loss of Helga was hard on them too, especially on Susanna who had been almost like a daughter to Helga. The four of us became very close. We had grown up together as children, but had lost touch for years. Now we were like sisters, which was wonderful.

On September 26th the Sundbyberg City Hall opened their permanent exhibition of Helga's sculptures and paintings. There was an abundance of people, flowers, champagne, and photos taken. It was the day before I left Sweden, and I was glad to be present.

During the trip home on the QE II, I often sat on deck and thought about Helga. I had already been in touch with her several times. The first time was three days after her death. Both Stu and I were awakened in the middle of the night by Helga "calling" us. We clearly perceived her presence, and a great love coming from her. Even in life, Helga had been a warm and cordial person, but this was something quite different. I think a person's body often prevents them from showing unrestrained love, as though the body cannot handle that much energy. Now that Helga's body was no longer in the way, she emanated a love so strong that both Stu and I were overwhelmed and wept with joy. These experiences helped me immensely in my grief and loss.

I gained a new and greater understanding of death. Through Helga I could feel what it is like to lose a body, to no longer be able to communicate in the usual way. I could see how the world looks when you cannot use the eyes of the body. It is clear that the personality survives death and can perceive events in the physical world. It is not hard to contact a dead person, especially if you have been close to them in life.

Helga and I began a new kind of relationship. It was no longer between an old and a younger person. No longer between mother and daughter. Helga was now a timeless being who had all ages at once. Mostly she was like a young girl, bright and shining and looking for new adventures.

EPILOGUE

There were many journeys. Good ones, bad ones, painful ones, joyous ones. All of them educational in some way or another, all part of my development as a human being.

The real journey is the spiritual one, the one towards personal freedom and integrity. I still have a long way to go on that one, but think I have taken a few important steps.

I know that another, higher reality exists, a different dimension than the one we see every day. I know that freedom and happiness are possible.

I feel it in those rare moments when another person actually sees me and talks to me. When someone truly loves me—not my body or some idea or image of me—but when they love *me*. When I love them the same way. In those moments I seem to step out of the physical universe.

I have experienced it in auditing, and when walking alone on the beach or in the mountains. Then I suddenly feel the presence of God.

In my nightly dreams, I sometimes find myself in fantastic landscapes or cities. They are a thousand times more beautiful than anything I have seen on earth. The colors are luminous and the bliss indescribable. I am weightless or floating in these dreams. Often one or several other beings are present, and the love between them and me is stronger than anything I have ever experienced in life. It is the same kind of love that I felt from Helga after her death. In my art I try to describe these feelings and paint these landscapes, but it is hard to do them justice.

Freedom comes when you forgive yourself and forgive others for past actions. When you know that your parents, cruel and crazy as they may have seemed, are not really to blame. Nobody ever taught them how to love and help children. They had their own problems and acted in the only way they could.

Tolerance and kindness work better than anything else. I wish a general amnesty could be declared, where we all forgive each other, and try to start over with a clean slate.

Made in the USA
Charleston, SC
02 April 2012